Chambers
card games for one

great games of patience

C014421873

CHAMBERS
An imprint of Chambers Harrap Publishers Ltd
7 Hopetoun Crescent
Edinburgh
EH7 4AY

www.chambers.co.uk

First published by Chambers Harrap Publishers Ltd 2008

© Chambers Harrap Publishers Ltd 2008

This book contains material previously published in *Chambers Card Games*
© Chambers Harrap Publishers Ltd 2007

Playing card images © Cut&Deal.com

All rights reserved. No part of this publication may be reproduced, stored in a retrieval
system or transmitted by any means, electronic, mechanical, photocopying or otherwise,
without the prior permission of the publisher.

We have made every effort to mark as such all words which we believe to be trademarks.
We should also like to make it clear that the presence of a word in this book, whether
marked or unmarked, in no way affects its legal status as a trademark.

A CIP catalogue record for this book is available from the British Library.

ISBN: 978 0550 10407 6

Hampshire County Library	
C014421873	
Askews	Oct-2008
795.4	£5.99
	9780550104076

Designed by Chambers Harrap Publishers Ltd, Edinburgh
Typeset by Gill McColl
Printed in Spain by Graphy Cems

Contents

Introduction......................................vii

Card Games

Accordion...3
Aces Up...5
As You Like It......................................7
Baker's Dozen......................................10
Baroness...13
Beleaguered Castle.................................14
Betsy Ross...16
Bisley...17
Bristol..19
British Blockade...................................21
British Square.....................................24
Calculation..26
Captive Queens.....................................29
Castles in Spain...................................31
Clock..33
Crossword..35
Demon..38
Duchess..41
Duchess de Luynes..................................43
Easthaven..45
Eight Off..47
Flower Garden......................................49
Fourteen Out.......................................52
Friday the Thirteenth..............................53
Frog...55
Gargantua..57
Gate...60
Grandfather's Clock................................63

Herringbone..65
King Albert..68
Klondike...71
La Belle Lucie.....................................73
Lady of the Manor..................................76
Lady Palk..79
Le Cadran..82
Legitimist...85
Limited..87
Little Spider......................................90
Martha...93
Matrimony..96
Miss Milligan......................................98
Monte Carlo.......................................101
Mount Olympus.....................................103
Odd and Even......................................106
One Foundation....................................108
Osmosis...110
Pas Seul..112
Perpetual Motion..................................113
Pyramid...115
Queen of Italy....................................117
Queen's Audience..................................120
Red and Black.....................................122
Rosamund's Bower..................................124
Royal Rendezvous..................................127
St Helena...129
Salic Law...131

Sir Tommy....................................133

Spider...135

Sultan...138

Tournament.................................140

Vacancies....................................143

Vanishing Cross...........................146

Weavers......................................148

Wheel of Fortune...........................152

Windmill......................................155

Card Games Glossary..........159

Index

Games by Alternative Names..........163

Games by Number of Packs............165

Introduction by Peter Arnold

Card games for one player (known as patience games in the UK and solitaires in the USA) are relative newcomers in the history of playing cards, yet today they probably outnumber all other card games.

The first collection of patience games to be published in English was *Illustrated Games of Patience*, compiled by Lady Adelaide Cadogan in around 1870 (the second edition was issued in 1874; the last remaining copy of the first edition was destroyed during World War II). It contained 24 games, most with French titles, and was probably translated from French sources. Some of the games featured are still played today. Prior to the appearance of Lady Cadogan's book, collections had been published in other countries, notably Sweden, Germany and Russia; the earliest known was published in Moscow in 1826.

There is evidence in 19th-century literature that card games for one were gaining in popularity. Both Tolstoy and Dostoevsky refer to patience games in their novels. Tolstoy, who was addicted to patience games, would sometimes base his solution to a problem on the outcome of a patience. He describes one such game in *War and Peace*, written in the 1860s, although the game in question was supposed to have been played in 1808. Dostoevsky, himself something of a mystic, has the wanton Grushenka calming herself with games of patience during a period of stress in *The Brothers Karamazov*, written in the 1880s. In addition, Charles Dickens mentions a patience game in *Great Expectations*, published in 1861 and thus predating Lady Cadogan's book.

Famous patience game enthusiasts include Albert, Queen Victoria's Prince Consort, and the US President Franklin D Roosevelt, who steadied his nerves in World War II by playing Spider (included herewith). But the list of addicts does not in all probability include Napoleon, whose association with the many games named after him, or after his island prison of St Helena, seems to have arisen from a case of mistaken identity.

Patience games are perhaps misnamed; although many certainly test patience, the absence of an opponent gives them more the nature of a puzzle than a game, particularly those which require skill. Those which depend entirely on luck are hardly games or puzzles, but merely pleasing ways of passing time. The satisfaction of success, or 'getting the game out', is nonetheless real, if illogical.

By far the most popular form of patience games is that where, from a dealt layout of cards called a 'tableau' (see Card Games Glossary, p159), the player must endeavour to 'build' cards in suit sequence on 'foundation cards' (frequently, but not always, Aces). Cards are manoeuvred around the tableau by 'packing' them onto each other, usually in descending order of sequence and by alternate colours. Klondike and Demon, probably the most-played forms of patience, are examples of this type of game.

Quite different types of patience games are those in which the cards are paired with each other (eg Fourteens), eliminated altogether (eg Perpetual Motion), built into a single pack (eg Accordion, Rosamund's Bower) or generally arranged in patterns (eg Captive Queens, Clock, Crossword).

This book contains as wide a variety of games as possible, with an indication given for each of the length of time it might take and the prospects of 'getting it out'.

All 65 games herewith are worth playing, and it is suggested that the reader might like to try them all, with the hope that some will become part of his or her repertoire. At the very least, playing an unfamiliar game with an unfamiliar layout does rule out that familiar pest who leans over the shoulder with the remark 'black 8 on red 9'.

Peter Arnold
London, March 2008

Card Games

Accordion

Accordion is the simplest of all patience games, so simple that it probably wasn't invented consciously but just evolved, or – more accurately – just happened. It has acquired the name Accordion because it takes place in one line of cards that during the game tends to get longer and shorter, rather like the way an accordion does when it is being played.

Alternative names	Idle Year, Methuselah
Number of packs required	One
Time needed to get it out	Six minutes
Prospects of success	About 1 in 60

Aim
To end with all 52 cards in one face-up pile.

Preparation
A single pack of cards is shuffled and held face down in the hand.

Play
Cards are turned over one at a time and played to the table. The first is dealt to the top left of the available playing space. The second card is played to its right and the third to the right of that and so on, so that the tableau, if it can be so called, is a single line of cards, or piles of cards.

A card that is played to the right of a card that it matches in either suit or rank can be packed upon it. Similarly, if a card matches in suit or rank a card third to its left, it can be packed upon it (ie the card will have to jump over two other cards). Those are the only two moves allowed. A move must always be made when possible. Sometimes a card can be packed in either of these two places, when the player must decide which of the two is preferable. Sometimes one move allows another, and the turn of one card might provoke several moves and shorten the 'accordion' accordingly.

When a card is the top card of a pile, then it governs the whole pile, and if it can be moved to the left it takes the whole pile with it – the pile should never be split. When a gap in the line is created by moving a card or pile forward along the line, then the card or cards to the right move to the left to close the gap. If the line gets so long that there is no space for further cards then a second line is started below the first, but the two lines must be considered as one continuous line.

The game ends when all the cards from the hand are dealt to the table. The game is won if there is only one pile on the table. If more, it is lost.

Accordion is a difficult game to win, and can be very frustrating, as you can approach the end with perhaps only three or four piles on the table and then deal seven or eight cards in a line, none of which can be moved.

Example game

Suppose there is a line of five piles, as illustrated.

Tableau

Next card

The next card turned up is the ♣9. The ♣9 is played to ♣7, and that pile played to ♦9. Then ♣K is played to ♣9 and then to ♠K. The accordion is then reduced to two piles, headed by ♣K and ♦3. If the next card is ♦K or ♣3, then the piles would be reduced to one. Notice, however, that if in the position shown, the ♣9 had been played to the ♣K instead of the ♣7, the only other move possible would have been ♣9 to ♦9, and the accordion would be left with four piles instead of two.

Aces Up

Aces Up is a simple and amusing game – that is if you consider it amusing to be foiled of success often by the very last cards you deal. It is a mechanical game of little skill (although mistakes are possible) but it pleasantly fills in any odd few minutes you may have to spare.

Alternative names	Firing Squad
Number of packs required	One
Time needed to get it out	Four minutes
Prospects of success	About one in eight

Aim
To discard all the cards except the four Aces.

Preparation
The cards are shuffled.

Play
Four cards are dealt in a row. If there is more than one card of a suit, the lower one is discarded (Ace ranks high, above King).

Another row of four cards is then dealt, overlapping the cards in the first row and filling any empty gaps, thus maintaining four piles. Again, any card lower in rank and of identical suit to another is discarded.

The game continues like this, with the player discarding a card whenever a higher card of the same suit is the exposed card on top of another pile. Any gap in the piles is filled, when possible, by any available card (ie the top card) from another pile. This may allow further moves before the next four cards are dealt. Obviously Aces cannot be discarded, as they are the highest cards, but when available they can be moved into a space created by all the cards in a pile being discarded.

The object is to discard all the cards, leaving just the four Aces on the table.

Strategy A player should not automatically play an Ace into a gap in the piles as soon as possible, although that is usually the best move. The cards need to be studied to work out what would happen if another available card were moved into the space. Sometimes a snarl-up can be eliminated by playing cards to gaps in a certain order.

Example game

In the game in progress illustrated, certain cards have already been eliminated, and the first column has been cleared. It would be a mistake to move the Ace immediately into the gap, as that would end the possible moves. Moving the ♠K into the gap, allows the ♦5 and then the ♠7 to be discarded, creating another space into which ♦A can be played. Each column now consists of one card, each of a differing suit, and the next four cards are dealt.

As You Like It

This is an unusual patience game that can become addictive. Its name is a mystery, there being no apparent connection with Shakespeare's play other than both require a little concentration, which is well repaid.

Alternative names	None
Number of packs required	Two
Time needed to get it out	25 minutes
Prospects of success	About 1 in 20

Aim
To finish with a row of eight 'index' cards, above each of which is a pile of twelve cards in ascending sequence, beginning with a card one rank above the index card and finishing with a card one rank below the index card.

Preparation
The two packs are shuffled together and taken face down into the hand.

Play
The first eight cards from the pack are dealt face down in a row. The player continues to deal cards face down upon them one at a time until all the cards are dealt, when there will be a row of eight piles each containing 13 cards. This is the tableau.

The top card of each pile is then turned over and placed face up above its pile. These are the index cards. It does not matter if two or more cards are of the same rank (although the chances are improved the fewer the duplicates). The eight piles of the tableau are then turned face up. The top card of each pile is available for play.

The foundations are cards one rank higher than the index cards, irrespective of suit. Any available face-up card in the tableau, one rank higher than an index card, is played to a position above the index card, from where it is built on in an ascending sequence, irrespective of suit, until the pile reaches the rank below the index card, when it is completed. The building on foundations is 'round the corner', ie when a King is reached it is followed by an Ace.

When all possible moves have been completed, the first pile (ie that on the extreme left) is picked up, turned face down in the hand, and then redealt face up one at a time to each of the eight piles, beginning at the left, and including any spaces which might have been created (including the one created by the pile being picked up).

Play proceeds as before and when all possible building has been completed the **second** pile is taken up and redealt, one to each pile, again beginning with the pile furthest left, and including the spaces. When play following the redeal of the second pile comes to an end, the **third** pile is redealt, and so on until all eight piles, if necessary, have been redealt. After that, if play once more comes to an end before all cards are played to foundations, the game is lost.

Cards may be played to foundations only at the completion of each redeal, ie they cannot be played while the redeal is taking place. It may be (especially near the beginning) that the redealt cards will supply one to all eight piles with some over to begin again at the left, while towards the end of the game the pile to be redealt may consist of one or two cards only (or even none at all).

Strategy In order to keep as many cards as possible in the piles to the right, it is best, where two cards of the same rank can be played to a foundation, to choose from a pile that has already been redealt. Although it is not strictly strategy, a good tip is to keep close watch on the index cards when building on foundations, since if a foundation is built on beyond its index card the game is ruined, and it is pointless to go further. Players who make this mistake more than once can be permitted to turn foundation piles face down when they are completed, thus removing the temptation to play on them further. Another easy but very annoying mistake is to build on an index card instead of the foundation.

Example game
The tableau piles were dealt, the index cards turned and placed in a row above them, and then the piles themselves turned over to give the situation in the illustration.

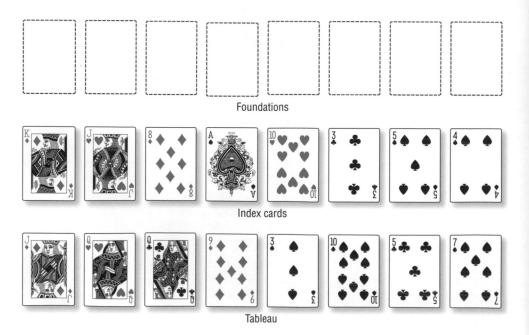

Foundations

Index cards

Tableau

The ♦J is played to the foundation row above the ♥10. (Note: it is not placed to cover the ♥10, which remains uncovered throughout to remind the player that the particular foundation pile is complete when it reaches a 9.) The ♥Q can be built on it and the ♣Q can be played to the foundation space above ♥J. The ♦9 is played to the foundation above the ♦8 and the ♠10 built upon it. The ♣5 can be played above the ♠4.

Thus six cards have been played to foundations and six more cards exposed, some of which might be playable to the foundations. At all times (except when there is a space in the tableau row) there are eight cards available for play.

Baker's Dozen

Since a baker's dozen is 13, and there are 13 cards to a suit, it was inevitable that sooner or later a patience game would adopt the expression. This one was very suitable, as the cards are all laid out in 13 columns at the beginning. A good game in which skill counts for as much as chance, skilful players can get it out more than half the time.

Alternative names	None, but a variant (see p12) is Good Measure
Number of packs required	One
Time needed to get it out	15 minutes
Prospects of success	About one in two

Aim
To finish with each suit in its own pile, built up in sequence from Ace to King.

Preparation
The pack is shuffled and dealt face up in four rows of 13 cards, each row overlapping the other (see illustration). All Kings are moved to the tops of their columns. Two or more Kings in the same column are each moved to the top. This is the tableau. There is no stock or waste heap.

Play
The bottom card of each column is available for play. As Aces become available, they are moved above the tableau to a foundation row, where they are built upon in suits in ascending order of rank up to the King. In addition to being built to the foundations, available cards can be packed on each other in descending sequence of rank, irrespective of suit, but only one at a time, ie a sequence cannot be moved from one column to another. A space caused by all the cards of a column being played is not refilled.

Example game
In the layout, as dealt, the Kings in columns 7 and 10 are removed and moved to the head of the columns. The ♠A is played to its foundation. The player must now by judicious moves release the other Aces to the foundations and build on them. If the reader lays out the cards as illustrated, the strategy section below will take him part way through the game.

Baker's Dozen

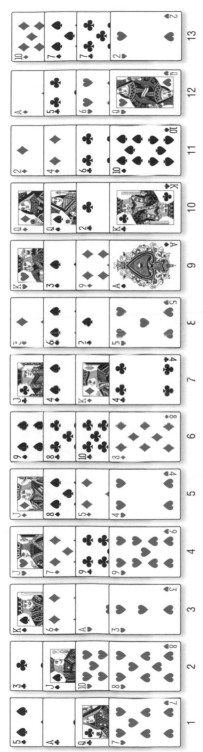

Foundations

Strategy The player can see where all the cards are so has his fate in his own hands. The problems lie when cards of the same suit appear in the same column with the higher card nearer the foot of the column. These 'reverses' must be overcome by manoeuvring cards around the tableau. This is more important than playing cards to the foundations, which can be done too quickly, since cards may be needed to resolve some of these foundations that might be needed to resolve some of these blockages. If possible, it is best to build on the foundations more or less equally. In the tableau as illustrated, after the ♦K and ♣K have been placed at the top of the columns, potential problems can be seen in reverses in columns 1 (♣A, Q), 3 (♥3, A), 6 (♣ 10, 8), 11 (♦4, 2) and 12 (♥Q, 6). The play might start: ♥3 to ♥4, ♥A to foundation, followed by ♥2, 3, 4, 5, ♠A to foundation, ♠8 to ♥9, ♦9 to ♠10, ♠2 and ♠3 to foundation, ♥7 to ♥8, ♠Q to ♥K, ♣A to foundation, followed by ♣2, ♦6 to ♥7, ♥Q to ♣K, ♥6 to foundation, ♣5 to ♣6, ♦A to foundation, ♦6 to ♣7, ♥7, 8 to foundation, ♦8 to ♦9, ♥9, 10 to foundation, ♠J to ♠Q, ♣3, 4, 5 to foundation, ♠10 to ♠J, ♣6 to foundation, 4 to ♦5, ♦2 to foundation, and so on. If the player now concentrates on releasing ♣8 from below ♣10, he will see this game comes out quite easily.

Variant

In the variant called Good Measure (a traditional Baker's Dozen can be said to be good measure, so the alternative title follows the same principle) the tableau consists of five rows of ten cards, the first two Aces to be dealt being placed straight to their foundations. From then on, the rules are the same, with the Kings being moved to the tops of their columns, etc. The length of the game, and its prospects of success, remain the same.

Baroness

Baroness is a most pleasant name for this ancient game, maintaining a tradition in which patience games were often named after ladies of the aristocracy. Its alternative names are merely the number of its piles and the target number that governs its play.

Alternative names	Five Piles, Thirteens
Number of packs required	One
Time needed to get it out	Five minutes
Prospects of success	About one in six

Aim
To remove all the cards from the tableau and discard them.

Play
Cards have their pip value, with King counting 13, Queen 12, Jack 11, and Ace one. The pack is shuffled well and taken into the hand. Five cards are dealt out in a row, to begin five piles. The five piles form the tableau. If any two cards have a combined pip value of 13 (eg Jack and 2, or 8 and 5), they are removed and placed to one side to start a discard pile. All Kings are added to the discard pile, since Kings count 13 on their own.

When any discards have been made, a further five cards are dealt to the tableau, either filling a gap in the row or being placed on a card already there. The top cards of each pile are now available for play. Any two whose pips total 13 (or Kings), are added to the discard pile. Another five cards are dealt to the piles, discards are made, and so on. When a card from a pile is discarded, the card below it becomes available.

After the final five cards are dealt, there will be two remaining, which are placed face up beside the tableau, in effect making a sixth and seventh pile. They are available for play. The game is won if all 52 cards are discarded.

Beleaguered Castle

Beleaguered Castle is a well established game for which a good deal of forward planning is usually required in order to get it out.

Alternative names	Laying Siege, Sham Battle
Number of packs required	One
Time needed to get it out	15 minutes
Prospects of success	About one in ten

Aim
To build each suit in sequence on its foundation from Ace to King.

Preparation
The four Aces are removed and placed in a column to the centre of the table. These are the foundations. A column of four cards is dealt to the left of the Aces, then a column of four cards to the right. Another column of four is built to the left, overlapping the first column, then a column to the right likewise, and so on alternately until all the cards are used and each side has four overlapping rows (see illustration).

Play
The cards at the outer end of each row, ie those not covered by other cards, are available for play. Each available card can be played in suit sequence to its foundation, or can be packed onto another available card in descending sequence, regardless of suit or colour. Only one card at a time can be played, ie sequences of cards cannot be moved from one tableau row to another. The playing of a card exposes the card below it which becomes available. A space created by all the cards in a row being played elsewhere is filled by any available card from another row.

Strategy This game requires some thought. Playing cards to foundations at the first opportunity is not the best way to proceed. It is more important, indeed necessary, to create spaces in the tableau to which cards that are blocking other rows can be played, and before playing any cards the player should try to plot a way to create a space. Thereafter, it is best to build foundations evenly to keep as many ranks as possible available in the tableau, which will help to create spaces.

Example game

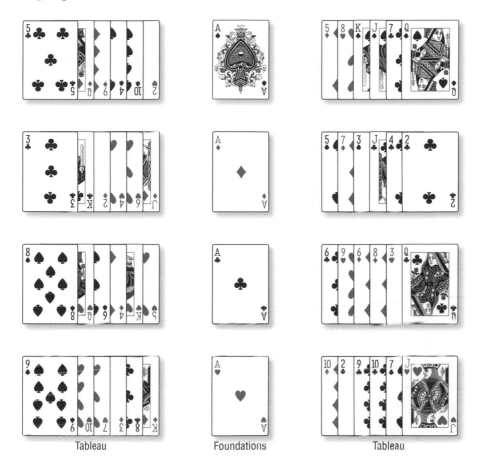

Tableau Foundations Tableau

The illustration shows the layout at the beginning of a game. The ♣2 is played to its foundation and play proceeds ♠8 to ♠9; ♥J to ♠Q; ♠7 to ♠8; ♣10 to ♥J; ♣9 to ♣10; ♠2 to foundation; ♣4 to ♣5; ♦10 to ♣J; ♣3 to foundation; ♣K to space.

By careful manipulation the second left-hand row can now be cleared, and play continues as described. This game was eventually got out.

Betsy Ross

Betsy Ross is a simple, short patience which requires little skill. It is not unlike Calculation (see p26).

Alternative names	Four Kings, Alliance, Musical Patience, Quadruple
Number of packs required	One
Time needed to get it out	Eight minutes
Prospects of success	One in eight

Aim
To build four foundations in different sequences up to Kings.

Preparation
Any Ace, 2, 3 and 4 are set out in a row, as shown in the illustration. Below them another row consists of any 2, 4, 6 and 8.

Play
The lower row comprises the foundations. The upper row is solely to indicate the different steps in which the foundations are to be built. Thus the first foundation is built in steps of one, regardless of suit or colour: 2, 3, 4, 5, 6, 7, 8, 9, 10, J, Q, K. The second is built in 2s: 4, 6, 8, 10, Q, A, 3, 5, 7, 9, J, K. The third is built in 3s: 6, 9, Q, 2, 5, 8, J, A, 4, 7, 10, K. The fourth is built in 4s: 8, Q, 3, 7, J, 2, 6, 10, A, 5, 9, K. The stock is taken in hand and cards turned over one at a time, and played to a foundation if possible. If not they are played to a single waste heap, the top card of which is always available for play. When the stock is exhausted two redeals are allowed, by the unshuffled waste heap being taken in hand face down and dealt twice more.

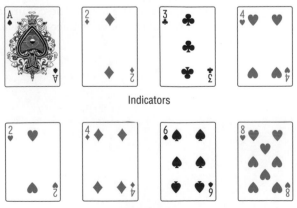

Indicators

Foundations

Bisley

Bisley takes up a lot of space, requiring a playing surface large enough for at least five rows of 13 cards. It lends itself to some skill, as choosing whether to pack up or down in the tableau can influence the outcome.

Alternative names	None
Number of packs required	One
Time needed to get it out	Eight minutes
Prospects of success	About one in two

Aim

To end with all the cards stacked in ascending suit sequences from the Aces upwards, or in descending suit sequences from the Kings downwards; it does not matter where the two sequences divide.

Preparation

The four Aces are placed in a row to the top left of the space for the tableau, leaving space for a row of cards above them. The remaining cards are shuffled and dealt face up, the first nine to the right of the Aces, and the rest in three rows of 13 beneath. An example layout is illustrated overleaf.

Play

All cards at the foot of a column are available for play or to be played on.

The Kings and Aces are foundations, and when Kings become available they are played to the space above their respective Aces. Cards available are played to their foundations, in ascending suit sequence on the Aces and descending suit sequence on the Kings.

In addition any available card can be played in ascending or descending suit sequence, according to choice, to cards at the foot of the columns. When a card is played from the foot of a column the card above it becomes available. A column which is cleared is not replaced.

Bisley

Example game

In the layout illustrated, the ♥2 and ♣2 can immediately be played to their respective Ace foundations, and the ♠K can be played to its foundation space above the ♠A. The ♥8 can be packed on ♥9, followed by ♥7 and ♥6, releasing the ♦K to be packed to its foundation spot. The ♦7 can be played to the ♦8, the ♠6 to the ♠5 and the ♣10 to the ♣9. This releases the ♠K to its foundation. The ♠10 can be packed on ♠9 and the ♣Q can be played to its King foundation. The ♥6, 7, 8, 9 can be packed on the ♥5, releasing ♠Q to its King foundation, and so on.

This example game can be got out if played carefully.

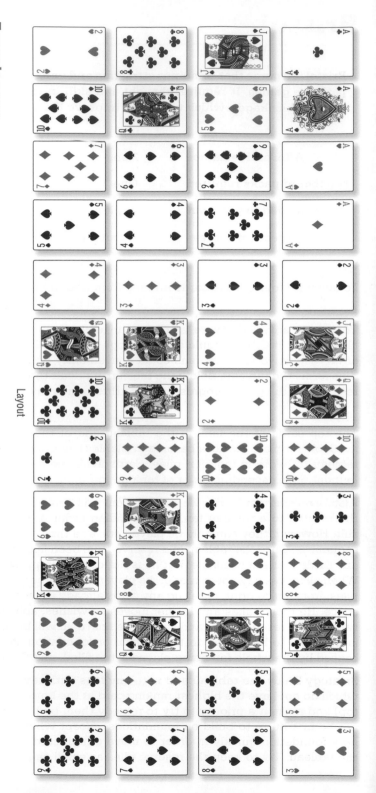

Layout

Bristol

Bristol is a game that combines attractive and unusual elements from other patience games. It requires thought and skill in managing the tableau to prevent blockages, which will much improve the prospects of success.

Alternative names	None
Number of packs required	One
Time needed to get it out	Eight minutes
Prospects of success	About one in four

Aim
To end with four piles of cards running from Ace to King, regardless of suit.

Preparation
The cards are dealt three at a time to eight fans of three cards each (see illustration). If a King should appear in one of the fans, it is moved to the bottom of its respective fan. The fans could conveniently be built in two rows of four. This forms the tableau. Below the tableau are dealt three cards face up to form a reserve. As the game progresses these three cards might become piles.

Play
The top cards of the fans in the tableau and of the reserve piles are always available for play. As Aces become available they are played to a row above the tableau to begin foundation piles. Cards available for play can be played to a foundation in ascending order of rank up to Kings, regardless of their suit.

Also, available cards can be played from one tableau fan to another, or from the reserve to a tableau fan, in descending order of rank, again regardless of suit. However, they can only be played one at a time – it is forbidden to transfer sequences. Once the tableau and reserve have been laid out, the player can move any cards that are available, but he is not obliged to make every move possible. When all moves have been made, the player deals three more cards to the reserve piles, from left to right, covering any cards already in the piles or filling an empty space. He then makes any further moves he wishes, and then deals three more cards to the reserve piles, and so on. The final deal will be of one card only, which is available to be played to the tableau or foundation. A space in the tableau caused by the whole fan being played is not filled, and there is no redeal.

Strategy Study the tableau and note any fans with reversed sequences (ie any which do not have the highest ranking card at the bottom, and the lowest at the top) and make it a priority to try to remedy them by building in the tableau. Do not be in a hurry to build on foundations, except when it is necessary to build up a foundation quickly in order to move a high card or two blocking a pile in the tableau. Try to keep the reserve piles as small as possible, and try to avoid reversed sequences in them. If Kings block any reserve pile it is necessary to build a foundation as soon as possible to get rid of the King. Do not empty a tableau fan unnecessarily, as this reduces the chances of playing a card from the reserve to the tableau, and of building in the tableau. In particular, do not play a lone King from the tableau to a foundation as a King in the tableau is useful for playing to it a Queen, which might otherwise block a reserve pile.

Example game

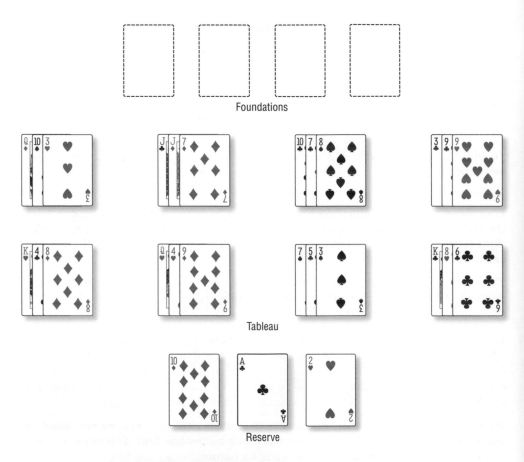

Foundations

Tableau

Reserve

In the illustration, the ♥K was dealt to the top of its fan, and then relocated to the bottom. There are four fans without a reversed sequence, which is better than can normally be expected. The three 9s are the biggest problem cards, since they block ♣3 and ♥4. The priority is to sort out the 9s, which would be helped if the two Jacks could be separated and the 10s played to them.

Play might proceed: ♣A to foundation, followed by ♥2 and ♥3. Then ♦9 to ♠10, ♠8 to ♦9, ♦7 to ♠8, ♥4 to foundation, ♦J to ♥Q, ♦10 to ♣J, ♥9 to ♦10. There is plenty of building possible yet, but at this stage it might be best to deal the next three reserve cards, and review the situation further.

ITEM RESERVATION SEND TO.
* *

HTH

* * * WRITE LOCATION CODE IN BOX ABOVE *

To   Hythe (Hythe)

* *

ITEM RESERVATION FOR COLLECTION
Res No . XXXX/ / 7
Name   : Haynes Raymond

Expires: 19 Jun 20 R
Notes :

* * * * * * * * * * * * * * * * * * * *

ITEM SENT FROM

Branch : Alton
Date   : 19/06/2017   Time :1630

Item   : C014421873
Chambers card games for 661

Haynes, R   7/7

HTH

British Blockade

British Blockade is an unusual and interesting patience game which unfortunately requires a lot of room, as the layout needs a space wide enough to take 13 cards and deep enough to take about six cards.

Alternative names	Parallels
Number of packs required	Two
Time needed to get it out	20 minutes
Prospects of success	About one in four

Aim
To build up four Aces in suit sequence to Kings, and four Kings down in suit sequence to Aces.

Preparation
Four Aces and four Kings (one from each suit in both cases) are removed from the combined pack and placed in two columns, Aces to the left and Kings to the right (with enough space between them to take a row of ten cards). These eight cards are the foundations.

The pack is shuffled and a row of ten cards dealt face up between the top Ace and top King. This forms the top row of the tableau.

Play
The object is to build up the Aces in suit sequence to the Kings and the Kings down in suit sequence to the Aces. The immediately available cards are all those dealt in the first row of the tableau. Any cards that can be built on the foundations are played there. The gaps created in the tableau are filled by turning over the stock one card at a time. The spaces must be filled from left to right.

When any subsequent building comes to a standstill and spaces are filled, a second row of ten cards is dealt from the stock below the first. The cards in both rows are available and building proceeds as before.

When play again comes to a standstill, a third row of cards is dealt. From here on the rules change – only the cards in the top and bottom rows are available. Those in the centre are blockaded, hence the name. However, the playing of a card from the top or bottom row makes a card in the middle row available. The rule is that to be available a card must have one of its shorter edges free, ie it must have one edge, either top or bottom, that is not adjacent to another card.

Play continues like this, with additional rows being dealt whenever play is blocked, until all cards are built on the foundations (success) or the stock is exhausted and no further building can be done (failure).

A summary of the rules is:

i) Only cards with a short side free are available for play.

ii) All vacancies must be filled at once when play comes to a standstill.

iii) Vacancies must be filled from left to right and top to bottom.

iv) A new row cannot be dealt until all vacancies are filled.

v) Cards cannot be built to foundations during the dealing of a row of ten.

vi) Building on a foundation is not compulsory.

vii) When the two foundation piles of a suit are in sequence (eg Ace is built up to 6 and King down to 7), cards may be reversed, ie switched from one pile to the other, provided the correct sequence is maintained. The Ace and King foundation cards cannot be reversed.

viii) A player is not allowed to look at the top card of the stock before deciding on a play.

Example game

The cards are dealt as in the illustration opposite. The ♣2 and one of the two ♣3s are built on the ♣A, the ♦Q is built on the ♦K, and the ♠Q is built on the ♠K. The four spaces created are filled from left to right from the top of the stock. If this enables other builds, they are then made and the spaces filled as before. When no other builds are possible, a second row of ten cards is dealt to the tableau, and play proceeds as described above.

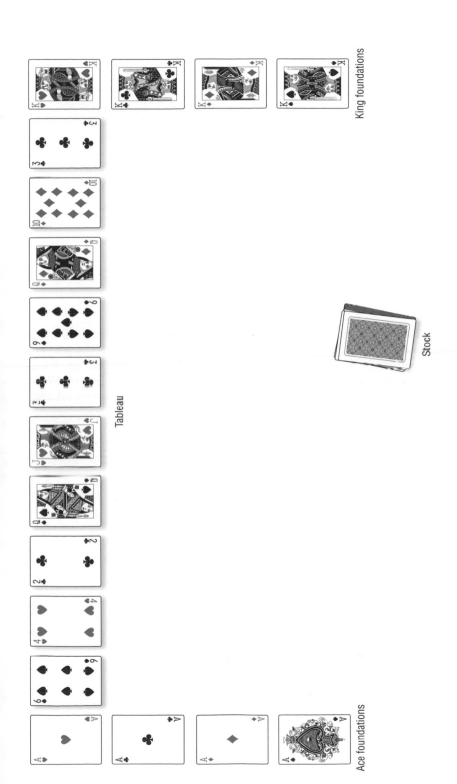

King foundations

Tableau

Stock

Ace foundations

British Square

British Square needs a moderately large space to play. It is an absorbing patience game, which requires care when packing on the tableau, but if the player retains his concentration, he will be successful much more often than not.

Alternative names	None
Number of packs required	Two
Time needed to get it out	15 minutes
Prospects of success	About three in four

Aim
To build up four Ace foundations in ascending order to Kings, and then the same foundations back down to Aces again.

Preparation
The combined pack is shuffled and 16 cards are dealt in four rows of four to form the tableau. There should be enough space between the rows to allow all 16 cards to be packed upon and the piles spread downwards. Space should also be left for four foundation piles, which might conveniently be beside the tableau (see illustration).

Play
As they become available, one Ace of each suit is played to a foundation space. The object is to build them up in suit sequence to Kings, then add the duplicate King, and build them down in suit sequence to Aces. Available cards are exposed cards in the tableau. As well as being built to foundations, they may be packed on each other in ascending or descending suit sequence. There are restrictions: only one card at a time can be moved from one tableau pile to another, not a whole sequence, and once the sequence is begun its direction cannot be changed. However, sequences can be reversed by playing the cards one at a time to another tableau pile, eg suppose a descending sequence is 9, 8, 7, 6, it can be reversed onto an available 5 on another pile, provided the 5 is alone or the end of an ascending sequence, by playing first 6, followed by the 7, 8, 9, to become an ascending sequence. Packing is not 'round the corner', ie a descending sequence ends with Ace and an ascending one with King.

When any building and packing has been completed from the initial tableau deal, spaces in the tableau are filled by turning cards over from the stock. When play is at a standstill, the stock is dealt one card at a time, and if a card cannot be played to foundation or tableau, it is played to a single waste heap, the top card of which is always available. Once a waste heap is established, spaces in the tableau can be filled from either the top of the waste heap or the stock, and the player may look at the next card of the stock before making his choice.

The game is won if all cards are dealt to the foundations and lost if the stock is exhausted beforehand and no further moves can be made. There is no redeal.

Strategy Care must be taken when building sequences on the tableau not to build duplicate cards in the same direction. In the first part of the game down-builds will be transferred first to foundations, and then when the two Kings are played, the up-builds can be played to foundations. Once a foundation is being built down to Ace, be careful not to have a down-build in the tableau that cannot be reversed.

Example game

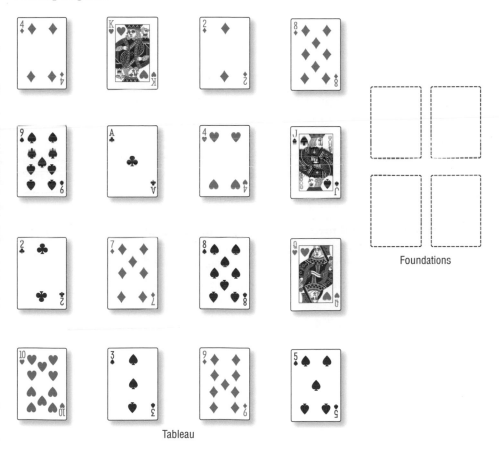

Foundations

Tableau

The illustration shows an initial deal. The ♣A is played to a foundation space and the ♣2 built on it. The ♦9 can have the ♦8 and 7 packed on it, the ♥Q can be packed on the ♥K and the ♠8 on the ♠9. The six spaces thus created are filled by the top six cards from the stock, there being no waste heap as yet. When all further moves are made, the first card is turned from stock and played to the foundation, tableau or waste heap. And so on.

Calculation

Calculation is a patience game with a deceptively simple layout. It is a difficult game to get out, but rewards careful play, and it is satisfying when what appears to be an unpromising situation suddenly comes to life and leads to success.

Alternative names	Broken Intervals
Number of packs required	One
Time needed to get it out	20 minutes
Prospects of success	About one in seven

Aim
To build all the cards into four piles upon foundations, each of which will be headed by a King.

Preparation
Cards rank from Ace (low) to King (high). Any Ace, 2, 3 and 4 are placed in a row on the table. They are the foundations. Below each foundation should be space for a waste heap.

Play
The pack is taken in hand face down and is dealt to the table one card at a time face up. A card may be played to a foundation, or to any waste heap. Cards should be played to the foundations to build sequences as follows.

The first pile begins with an Ace, and is built on in the order, irrespective of suits: A, 2, 3, 4, 5, 6, 7, 8, 9, 10, J, Q, K

The second pile begins with a 2, and is built on in intervals of two:
2, 4, 6, 8, 10, Q, A, 3, 5, 7, 9, J, K

The third pile begins with a 3, and is built on in intervals of three:
3, 6, 9, Q, 2, 5, 8, J, A, 4, 7, 10, K

The fourth pile begins with a 4, and is built on in intervals of four:
4, 8, Q, 3, 7, J, 2, 6, 10, A, 5, 9, K

The top card of a waste heap is always available to play to a foundation, but it may not be played to another waste heap. The cards on the waste heaps can be slightly overlapping, so that the ranks of the cards below the top one can be seen.

The pack is dealt once only, although play may continue to be made from waste heaps so long as there is a card to be played to a foundation. If the pack is exhausted and none of the cards on the top of the waste heaps may be played to a foundation the game is lost.

Strategy The skill lies in deciding on which waste heap to lay a card which cannot be played to a foundation. An attempt should be made to build up runs in the waste heaps of cards at intervals of one, two, three or four to each other, so that when a card will eventually fit on a foundation, others will follow.

Example game

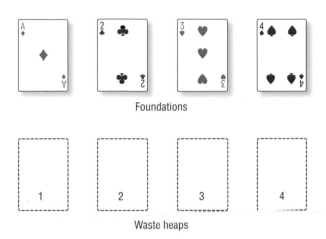

Foundations

Waste heaps

Suppose the first card turned up from the pack is a 9. Place this on the space for the first waste heap. The next card is a Queen. Place this on the second waste heap space. The next card is a 2. This is played to the Ace foundation. The next card is a 3, which also goes on the Ace foundation. Next another 3. This will not be needed for some time, so can go on waste heap 3. The next card is a 5, which can be played to waste heap 3. The next card is a King. As Kings end at the top of all the foundation piles, they will be among the last to be played, and it is as well to reserve a waste heap for these, so place it on waste heap 4. The next card is a Queen, which can go onto the waste heap 2 above the other Queen. The next card is 8, which goes to the 4 foundation, followed by the Queen from waste heap 2. The next card dealt is a 6. This is played to the 3 foundation, followed by the 9 from waste heap 1 and the other Queen from waste heap 2. The next card dealt, a Jack, is played to waste heap 1, where it might remain for a little while.

The next card is a 4. This will fit onto either the Ace or 2 foundations. The best play would be to play it to the Ace foundation, since this will allow the 5 on waste heap 3 to follow onto the Ace foundation, uncovering the 3 to go on the 4 foundation. The next card is 7 which also goes onto the 4 foundation, allowing the Jack from waste heap 1 to follow it. The next card is 2, which fits onto the 3 foundation. As the game progresses, 9 goes to waste heap 1, a 10 to waste heap 2, a Queen to waste heap 3, a King to waste heap 4, an Ace to waste heap 1, a 5 to the 3 foundation, a Jack to waste heap 3, a 4 to the 2 foundation, an 8 to the 3 foundation, followed by the Jack from waste heap 3 and the Ace from waste heap 1, and so on.

As the game stands, a 6 is needed for the Ace and 2 foundations, a 4 for the 3 foundation and a 2 for the 4 foundation. This is a very good start and very few games will go as smoothly as this. Any reader who has followed with a pack of cards can shuffle the remaining cards and, dealing them one by one, see how much further the game can progress.

Captive Queens

Captive Queens is a similar game to Quadrille, and the two are often confused. Captive Queens is preferred for this book because of the very attractive tableau a successful game makes. Also, it is surprising how often the game is winnable, however bleak the prospects might appear halfway through the second and final redeal.

Alternative names	None
Number of packs required	One
Time needed to get it out	Six minutes
Prospects of success	Two in five

Aim
To finish with a tableau showing the four Queens intertwined in the centre, each one guarded by two piles of cards, one headed by her King and the other by the Jack.

Preparation
The four Queens are extracted from the pack and intertwined in the centre of the table as shown in the illustration overleaf.

Play
The cards are shuffled, and dealt one by one to the table. As the 6s and 5s are turned up they are placed one to each side of the Queen of their respective suit. Other cards are played to a waste heap. The 6s and 5s are foundations, and as soon as a 6 or 5 is in position it can be built upon. The top card of the waste heap is available for building. The 6 is built upwards to the Jack, ie 7, 8, 9, 10, Jack. The 5 is built down to the King, with King following Ace, ie 4, 3, 2, Ace, King.

When the stock is exhausted (all the foundation cards will be in position) it is turned over and, without being shuffled, dealt again, with the foundations being built on further. Hardly ever is the game got out on this redeal, and there is usually quite a substantial waste heap after it. This is turned over again, without shuffling, and redealt a second and final time. It is surprising how successful this redeal often is, and in nearly half of games the waste heap will disappear altogether, leaving the pleasing conclusion where the only cards to be seen are the twelve court cards looking up from the tableau.

Example game

The illustration shows a game in progress about halfway through the first deal. The ♥5, ♣6, ♦5, ♦6 and ♠6 have already been dealt and played to their foundations. The ♠7 has also been dealt and built on ♠6, and both the ♦4 and ♦3 have been dealt and built on the ♦5.

Castles in Spain

Castles in Spain is a simple patience game with an attractive layout suitable for those players with 10 or 15 minutes to spare and who want to be sure of getting the game out at least once.

Alternative names	None
Number of packs required	One
Time needed to get it out	Six minutes
Prospects of success	About nine in ten

Aim

To finish with four piles of 13 cards, one for each suit, the cards being in ascending sequence from Ace to King.

Preparation

From a shuffled pack, five cards are dealt face down in a row with double spaces between them. Above the spaces a row of four cards is dealt, then a row of three cards and then a single card above the rest. The shape roughly resembles a castle with a tower. A second card is dealt face down on each, and then a third. Finally a card is dealt face up to each pile. This forms the tableau (see illustration overleaf).

Play

The face-up card of each pile is available for play. Aces, as they become available, are played to the centre as foundations, to be built on in ascending suit sequence to the Kings. Otherwise, cards can be packed from one pile in the tableau to another, in descending sequence of alternate colours. When a card is played from a pile the face-down card below it is exposed and becomes available for play. When a space is created by a whole pile being played either to foundations or elsewhere in the tableau, it is filled by an available card, or sequence, from another tableau pile.

Strategy As soon as an Ace or two is played to a foundation, or a space created in the tableau, the game is almost certain to be got out. Spaces in the tableau should be filled by high cards rather than, for example, 2s. Should a game fail it is likely to happen almost immediately (it is possible that on the initial deal no available cards can be moved).

Example game

Foundations

Tableau

The cards are dealt as in the illustration. The ♦A is played to a foundation space, and the ♦2 built on it. The cards below are then turned face up and become available for play. The ♥5 is packed on ♣6, and ♣4 follows it, making two more cards available. The ♠J is packed on the ♥Q, and the card below turned over. When the new cards become available they are built to foundations, or packed on the tableau, or are themselves packed on, and so the game continues.

Clock

There are two patience games with a clock layout in this book (see also Grandfather's Clock, p63): this is the simpler, and is a good game for a child learning to tell the time. It is a game very rarely got out, and depends entirely on chance, but a child should turn up at least one card for each number on the dial, which may be sufficient to please.

Alternative names	Sundial, Travellers
Number of packs required	One
Time needed to get it out	Five minutes
Prospects of success	About 1 in 60

Aim
To end with every card turned face up in piles by rank, laid out in the form of a clock face.

Preparation
A large playing area is needed. The cards are shuffled and dealt to a tableau in the form of a clock face: twelve packets of four cards are dealt face down to positions representing the twelve numbers on the dial. It does not matter whether the cards are dealt one at a time to each position in turn, or in batches of four. A final packet of four is placed in the centre of the clock face.

Play
Play begins with the top card of the centre packet being turned over and placed face up on the outside of the packet on the clock face which represents the number of the rank of the card. For example, a 3 of any suit would be placed face up outside the packet at the three o'clock position on the dial. An Ace represents 1 o'clock, a Jack 11 o'clock and a Queen 12 o'clock. A King which is turned up is placed face up next to the packet in the centre.

When a card has been played to its spot on the dial or the centre, the top card is taken from the face-down packet in that position and played in turn to its appropriate position, with a card being taken from there and played to its spot, and so on. The illustration overleaf shows a game in progress.

The game ends in failure if the fourth King appears before all the numbers on the clock face are filled with face-up cards, because when the fourth King appears and is played to the middle there are no more face-down cards there with which to carry on the game. The game is won if every card gets turned face up (ie, if the final card to be turned face up is the fourth King).

Example game

The illustration shows a game in progress. Every spot on the dial has had at least one card played to it.

The last card to be played was the ♠3, and the player takes the top face-down card from the pile at 3 o'clock and plays it to its position, taking the next card from there, and so on.

Crossword

Crossword is a patience game invented by the late George F. Hervey, author of books and hundreds of newspaper and magazine columns on cards. Its tableau resembles the grid of a crossword. It is a skilful game, which is usually determined on the turn of the final two or three cards.

Alternative names	None
Number of packs required	One
Time needed to get it out	Ten minutes
Prospects of success	About one in two

Aim
To complete a 7 x 7 card tableau where the face-up cards in each column and in each row add up to an even number.

Preparation
Cards count their pip value, Ace being one. The twelve court cards are removed from the pack and put aside face down for the time being. These will represent the black squares of the crossword.

Play
The remaining 40 cards are shuffled and taken in hand face down. The top card is turned up from the hand and played to the table. The next and subsequent cards in turn are played to the table in a position adjoining a card already played, either adjacent to one side, or to top or bottom, or diagonally, ie corner to corner.

The object is to build up a square of seven cards by seven, using, at will, the face-down cards to represent the black squares in a crossword, so that each run of face-up cards, running from left to right or top to bottom, totals an even number, even if it is only one card in a row, as the ♣10 is in the illustration of a completed game overleaf, or a single card in a column (♠2, ♣6, ♠6, ♥4 in the illustration).

When there is only one square in the grid to fill, the player may look at all four cards remaining (either in hand or among the 'black' squares) and choose which to play.

Strategy It is a mistake to regard the cards representing black squares as cards to fall back upon if one is in a fix. At least nine of them have to be used in the completed square, and the chances of success are improved if they are used uniformly throughout. It is usually best to play odd-numbered cards away from the edges of the square, since they cannot be isolated there, as the ♣10, ♠2 and ♠6 are in the illustration of a successful ending to a game. An odd-numbered card must have another card adjacent top or bottom and to one of its long sides. It is generally best to build up the square outwards from the centre, leaving the corners till last. But the attraction of this patience game is that those who try it will work out their own ways to overcome its problems. The illustration of a successful outcome to a game shows that all the face-up cards were included, the three cards not used being those representing black squares. Notice that a black square could have been used in place of any of ♦6, ♣6, ♦10, ♣8, ♠2, ♦8, ♦4, ♥4, ♠8, ♥6. A beginner will probably not get one of two games out, but an experienced player will better this.

Demon

Demon and Klondike (see p71) are the best-known games of patience. Both are often called Canfield in the UK and the USA, although the name is properly attached only to Demon. This is because it was said to have been invented by a famous US gambler and casino owner of the 19th and early 20th centuries, William A. Canfield, who would 'sell' the pack to a punter for $52 ($1 per card) and pay out $5 for each card in the foundation row at the end of the game. While a player can frequently obtain the eleven cards necessary in the foundation row to make a profit from Mr Canfield, it is a difficult game to get out entirely.

Alternative names	Canfield, Thirteen
Number of packs required	One
Time needed to get it out	Ten minutes
Prospects of success	About 1 in 30

Aim
To end with four piles of cards, one for each suit, in sequence.

Preparation
Thirteen cards are dealt face down in a pile, and the top card of the pile is turned face up. This pile is known as the 'heel'. The next four cards are dealt face up in a row to the right of the heel to form the tableau. The next card is dealt face up above the first card of the tableau. This is the first foundation card, and decides the rank of all the other foundation cards. The remaining cards form the stock.

Play
The other three cards of the foundation rank should be played in a row to the right of the first foundation card as they become available. These cards will be built up in suit and ascending sequence until all the cards in the pack are built on the foundations. The sequence is 'round-the-corner', ie Queen, King, Ace, 2, 3 and so on.

The exposed cards on the heel and the bottoms of the columns of the tableau are all available to play. Once all available moves have been made, the stock is taken face down in hand and turned over in bundles of three, without disturbing their order, to a waste pile, or 'talon'. The top card of the talon is now also available to play to the foundations or tableau. Cards are played to the tableau in columns in descending order of rank and in opposite colours, for example ♥4 or ♦4 may be played on ♠5 or ♣5. These sequences are also round-the-corner, so if an Ace is at the foot of a column, a King of the opposite colour can be played to it.

A whole column in the tableau may be transferred to another provided the sequence is maintained, for example a column headed by ♥8 or ♦8 can be transferred to a column ending with a ♠9 or ♣9. An emptied tableau column is filled immediately by the top card of the heel, the next card in the heel then being turned face up. If the heel becomes exhausted, an empty column is filled by an exposed card from the talon, but this need not be done immediately – one may wait until a more useful card is exposed.

When the whole stock has been played to the talon (the last bundle may be of only one or two cards), and all possible moves have been completed, the talon is picked up and turned over without rearrangement and is again played to the table as before in bundles of three. The game ends in success when all cards are built to the foundations; in failure when the whole stock has been played to the talon without it being possible to play a card to tableau or foundation.

Example game
The heel, foundation card and tableau are dealt as illustrated.

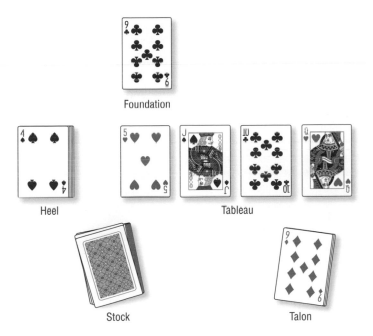

Foundation

Heel   Tableau

Stock   Talon

The play then begins with the ♠4 being built from the heel onto the ♥5, and the next card of the heel being faced. The ♣10 is then built on to the ♣9 in the foundation row and is replaced by the second card of the heel, the third card then being faced. The ♠J is built onto the ♥Q and its place in the tableau filled by the next card from the heel. The cards played from the heel may themselves offer chances to build further.

When all activity is over, the stock is taken in hand and the first bundle of three cards played to the table to begin the talon, as shown. The first card exposed is the ♦9, which being a foundation card is played to the foundation row to the right of the ♣9, and the ♦10 and then later diamonds are played to it as they become available. If the card in the talon exposed by the moving of the ♦9 will fit into the tableau or foundation row, it is moved there. If not, the next bundle of three cards are turned from the stock onto the talon, and any possible moves made, and so on.

Variant

A popular variant to this game is that instead of dealing a card to the foundation row to determine the rank of the foundations, the foundations are always the Aces (as they are in many patience games). Only eleven cards are dealt to the heel, and the top card is not faced. The heel is used only to supply a card to a column in the tableau which becomes empty, and only then is the card turned face up. Aces are played to the foundation row as they are exposed (either in the original four cards to the tableau, or as the top card in the waste pile, or as the card turned up from the heel to fill a gap in the tableau).

Duchess

Duchess is a patience game in which the player can choose from four cards to indicate the rank of the foundations, and also has choices to fill the tableau. It makes for an interesting game with a fair chance of a favourable outcome.

Alternative names	Glenwood
Number of packs required	One
Time needed to get it out	Ten minutes
Prospects of success	About one in eight

Aim
To build up the foundations in suit sequence.

Preparation
The cards are shuffled and four fans of three cards each are dealt at the top of the available space. These fans form the reserve. Space is left below these for a row of four foundations, and below this space is dealt a row of four face-up cards to form the tableau.

Play
The top cards of the four fans are always available for play to foundations or tableau, and the first task of the player is to choose one as the rank of the foundations and to move it into the foundation row.

The object is to play the other cards of the foundation rank to the row as they become available and build upon them in ascending 'round the corner' suit sequence (ie Ace following King and preceding 2) until the whole of each suit is played to the foundations.

Cards available for play are the cards exposed in the tableau. Tableau cards can also be packed upon each other in descending order of alternate colours, a whole sequence being moved as a single unit. Packing on tableau piles is not 'round-the-corner', and ends with an Ace.

When a space occurs in a tableau column, it is filled by any available card from the reserve, or, when the reserve is exhausted, by the top card of the waste heap.

The stock is dealt one card at a time, and cards which cannot be built to a foundation or packed on the tableau are played to a waste heap, the top card of which is always available. When the stock is exhausted, and play is at a standstill, one redeal is allowed. The waste heap is turned over without shuffling to provide the new stock.

Example game

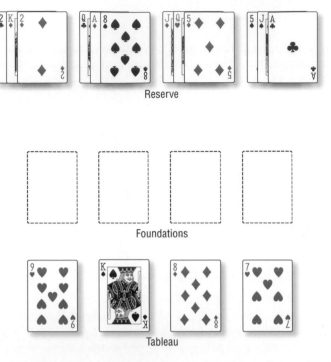

Reserve

Foundations

Tableau

The four fans and the tableau are dealt as in the illustration. The first thing the player must do is choose the foundation rank. Although the ♠8 would immediately be joined by ♦8 from the tableau, the best choice is ♣A, which opens developments. The ♠8 is packed on the ♥9 in the tableau, and the ♥7 is packed on the ♠8. The ♦A is released to the foundation row, and the ♦2 built on it. The ♦K can fill the space in the tableau, and the ♣Q packed on it. The ♣2 is thus released to the foundation row. It is an excellent start. The first card is now turned from the stock.

Duchess de Luynes

The Duchess de Luynes, yet another noble lady associated with patience games, gives her name to a popular game which rewards luck rather than skill. However, the mechanics of it require some concentration.

Alternative names	Grand Duchess (with variation Parisienne, Parisian)
Number of packs required	Two
Time needed to get it out	16 minutes
Prospects of success	About one in twelve

Aim

To have each suit built up in two piles, one in ascending sequence from Ace to King, and the other in descending sequence, King to Ace.

Preparation

The two packs of cards should be thoroughly shuffled. The combined pack is taken in hand face down, although to start dealing it is usual and convenient to split the pack roughly into two, since 104 cards may be difficult to manage. Only four cards are dealt face up to the table to form the tableau, plus two cards face down to start a reserve. Room for two rows of cards must be left above the tableau for the ascending and descending foundations (see illustration).

Play

The four cards in the tableau are available for play. As the game progresses these cards will be added to to form piles, and the top cards of the piles are available for play.

If the initial four cards dealt contain any Aces or Kings, they are automatically moved to the foundation rows (Aces top row, Kings second row). They are not replaced, but the spaces are filled as the stock is played.

As play progresses, Aces and Kings are played to the foundation rows until the rows contain one Ace and one King of each suit. As soon as the foundation cards are played, available cards can be built on them by suit, 2s up to Kings on the Aces, and Queens down to Aces on the Kings.

Once the tableau is in place, four more cards are dealt face up on the original four, plus two more face down to the reserve. When those six cards are dealt, available cards are built to the foundations, if possible. Play continues in this way until the stock is exhausted (it is likely that a foundation space or two will still be empty).

When the stock is exhausted, the reserve is taken in hand, fanned out, and cards from it played to the foundations where possible. While this progresses, available cards from the tableau (ie those on the top of the four piles) can continue to be played to the foundations.

When all possible building has been completed, three redeals are allowed. The four tableau piles are picked up, face up, from left to right, the leftmost being placed on its right-hand neighbour, the combined pile onto the third pile and then onto the fourth. The reserve is placed face up on top, and the whole pile turned over to form the new stock. This is then dealt in exactly the same way as before, with four cards being dealt face up, and two face down to form the new reserve, with available cards being built to the foundations where possible. The same procedure is used to form the stock for the third deal. On the fourth deal, however (the third redeal), cards are not dealt to a reserve pile. In this deal, if the stock is exhausted before all cards are built to foundations, the game has failed.

It is important that during the deals, cards are not played to the foundations until the deal is complete, ie until cards have been dealt to all four piles in the tableau, and, in the first three deals, two face down to the reserve.

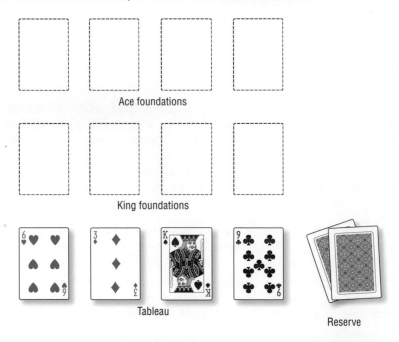

Ace foundations

King foundations

Tableau

Reserve

The illustration shows an initial deal. The ♠K is played to its foundation, the only move that can be made. Four face-up cards are now dealt to the four tableau piles, including one to the space, and two more to the reserve, and so the game continues.

Variant
In the variant called Parisienne, or Parisian, one Ace and one King of each suit are removed from the pack in advance and placed in position as foundations. This slightly improves the chances of getting the patience out. Some players prefer that at each redeal the stock is shuffled, but this does not necessarily improve the game.

44

Easthaven

Easthaven is an infuriating game if it fails almost before it begins, but can be very satisfying when it succeeds with a rush, as it often does, from very unpromising situations. Easthaven is also known as Aces Up, though this name has been used for another game in this book.

Alternative names	Aces Up
Number of packs required	One
Time needed to get it out	Six minutes
Prospects of success	One in five

Aim
To end with four piles of cards, one for each suit, running in sequence from Ace up to King.

Preparation
The cards are shuffled and a row of seven dealt out face down to the table. A second card is dealt face down to each of these, then a third card face up. The tableau thus consists of seven piles of three cards, two face down and the top card face up.

The cards at the top of each pile are available for play. Aces, when available, are moved to a foundation row above the tableau and are built on in suit sequence up to the Kings.

The tableau can be packed upon by packing down in alternate colours. The top card of a pile, or a sequence, can be moved to the top of another pile, providing the correct downward sequence of alternating colours is maintained. The top cards of the piles are always available to build to a foundation. When an available card sequence is moved to a foundation or to another tableau pile, exposing a face-down card, that card is turned face up and becomes available.

If a space occurs in the tableau because the whole pile has been moved, the space can be filled from the tableau, but only by an available King, or by a sequence build headed by a King. Otherwise it is filled in the normal course of dealing. When all moves have been made in the tableau, another row of seven cards is dealt face up to the existing piles, and play proceeds as before. It is not compulsory to make all possible moves in the tableau before a new row of cards is dealt (although usually advisable) except that a space must be filled (if possible) before a new row is dealt.

On the last deal there will be only three cards remaining, which are dealt to the first three piles.

Example game

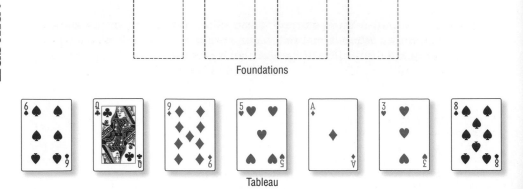

Foundations

Tableau

The initial tableau is dealt as in the illustration. The ♦A is played to a foundation space, exposing the face-down card below it, which is turned face up and becomes available, ♥5 is played to ♠6, and ♠8 is played to ♦9, thus exposing two more cards to be turned face up. Further moves, if possible, are made with the new cards exposed, and when play comes to a standstill, a further seven cards are dealt face up, and play resumes.

Eight Off

Eight Off is a fascinating patience game, often providing many choices of play at various points. For this reason it rewards careful play, and the skilful player should expect to succeed half the time.

Alternative names	Eight Away
Number of packs required	One
Time needed to get it out	15 minutes
Prospects of success	About one in two

Aim
To build up each suit in sequence from Ace to King.

Preparation
The pack is shuffled and a row of eight cards is dealt face up to the table. On these cards five further rows of eight cards are dealt, each overlapping the card before, so that the tableau consists of eight columns of six overlapping cards, all face up. The remaining four cards in the pack are dealt in a row below the tableau to form a reserve. Above the tableau are four spaces to which the Aces will be played as foundation cards as they become available (see illustration overleaf).

Play
All the cards fully exposed at the bottom of each column are available for play, as are all the reserve cards. They can be built on the foundations in ascending suit sequence from Ace to King, or packed upon another available card in the tableau in descending suit sequence. However, cards can be plucked from the tableau only one at a time, ie a sequence cannot be moved as a unit from one tableau column to another. If a space occurs because all the cards in a column have been played, it can be filled by a King, but only an available King.

The game gets its name from the reserve. Cards can be played from the tableau to the reserve, provided that the reserve never exceeds eight cards. It is in the manipulation of the tableau by playing cards in and out of the reserve that the skill of the game lies.

Strategy The reserve is valuable and spaces in it should be used in order to unblock cards in the tableau columns. For example, if the ♥3 can be played to the foundation but it is buried in a column beneath the ♣9, by playing the ♣9 to the reserve, the ♥3 is released for the foundation. The reserve should not be completely filled unless doing so immediately releases cards from the tableau, which will also allow cards to be played from the reserve. Keeping spaces available in the reserve is more valuable than creating them in the tableau.

Example game

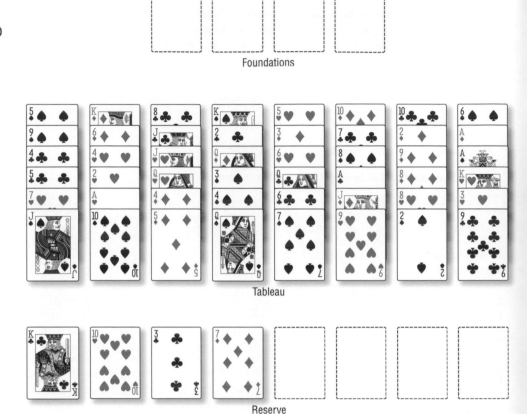

Foundations

Tableau

Reserve

The cards are dealt as in the illustration. An urgent task is to release the two Aces in the right-hand column to the foundation, which need not necessarily involve creating a space in the tableau first in which to play the ♥K. Play might proceed as follows: ♠10 packed on ♠J; ♥A and ♥2 to foundation; ♣9 to reserve; ♥3 to foundation; ♥K to reserve; ◆A and ♠A to foundations; ♠6 to ♠7; ♥K to tableau space; ♥4 to foundation; ◆5 to ◆6; ◆4 to ◆5; ♥Q to ♥K; ♥J to ♥Q; ♥10 from reserve to tableau; ♥9 to ♥10; ◆J to reserve; ♣A to foundation… and so on. This game eventually came out very easily.

Flower Garden

Flower Garden has been a popular patience game for a long time, perhaps because of its romantic terminology, the columns of cards being called flower beds, the tableau the garden and the reserve the bouquet. However, getting the game out is not all roses; it takes skill not to end with a heap of weeds.

Alternative names	Bouquet, The Garden
Number of packs required	One
Time needed to get it out	15 minutes
Prospects of success	About one in three

Aim

To end with four piles of cards, one for each suit, in sequence from Ace up to King.

Preparation

A large surface is required. Six rows of six cards are dealt face up, making six overlapping columns (see illustration overleaf). Traditionally they are dealt in fans, but the columns are easier to manipulate. These columns are known as the 'beds'. The remaining 16 cards are arranged in a crescent above them. This is the 'bouquet'. The four blank spaces are the foundations where the Aces will go when they become available.

Play

Aces should be released from the bouquet and, as they become available for play, from the beds. They should be placed in a row above the bouquet as foundations, and built upon in ascending suit sequences to the Kings.

All the cards at the foot of the beds and all the cards in the bouquet are exposed and are available for play. They may be built on the foundations as they become available, or may be packed on the exposed card at the foot of a bed in descending sequence, irrespective of suit or colour. A sequence may be moved from the foot of one bed to another provided the sequence is retained. If a bed is cleared, the vacant space may be filled either with an exposed card or sequence from another bed, or with a card from the bouquet.

Strategy The game can be difficult to get out if there are Aces and other low cards buried at the top of the beds and court cards, particularly Kings, at the base of the beds. The main aim is to release the Aces, 2s and 3s and to try to clear beds in order to fill the space with any Kings which are blocking cards in the beds they occupy. Packing a card from the bouquet on to a bed should be avoided if possible as it reduces the number of cards that can be played at any time, but it is sometimes necessary.

Flower Garden

Foundations

Bouquet

Beds

50

Example game

The bouquet and beds are as shown in the illustration opposite. It looks quite promising. The first tasks are to try to release the ♥3 from the head of the sixth bed and to transfer the ♥K, ♥Q, ♥J from the fourth bed to the head of the sixth.

The ♠A and ♥A can be moved from the bouquet to a row above as the first two foundations. Play might then proceed: ♥2 to foundation; ♠5 packed on ♥6; ♠2 to foundation; ♦3 packed on ♦4; ♣8 packed on ♦9; ♣A to foundation; ♦4, ♦3 packed on ♠5; ♥8 packed on ♠9; ♥3 to foundation; ♠7 packed on ♥8; ♦9, ♣8 packed on ♥10; ♥K to head of the empty sixth bed; ♥4 to foundation; ♦A to foundation; ♣2 to foundation; ♦2 from bouquet to foundation; ♦3 followed by ♦4 to foundation; ♥Q, ♥J packed on ♥K; ♠3 to foundation; and so on.

This game is progressing well. Readers who have set it up to follow it can play on. They will find that it comes out quite easily. The original layout is rarely as favourable as it was here, with two Kings nicely tucked away at the head of a bed where they were unable to block the play.

Variations

The bouquet cards may be held in the player's hand, rather than laid out. The beds may also be arranged on the table in fans, rather than in rows, with the exposed card on the right-hand of each fan available for play.

Fourteen Out

Fourteen Out is a simple patience game, which can usually be got out with a little concentration. It is a game in which cards are removed in pairs until the table is cleared.

Alternative names	Fourteens, Take Fourteen
Number of packs required	One
Time needed to get it out	Five minutes
Prospects of success	About two in three

Aim
To clear all the cards off the table to a waste heap.

Preparation
The cards are shuffled and a face-up row of twelve cards is dealt. Overlapping it are three more rows of face-up cards. The remaining four cards are dealt one each to the first four columns.

Play
The cards at the foot of each column are available for play. Any two, the pips of which total 14 (Ace counting one, King 13, Queen twelve and Jack eleven), can be removed and discarded to a waste pile, exposing two more cards available for play. A space caused by a column of cards being played is not refilled. If all cards can be disposed of in this manner the game is won.

Strategy If a game fails it is likely to fail early, simply because no two cards at the foot of the columns 'match', ie their total pips add up to 14. Otherwise the main hindrance to getting the game out is the appearance of matching cards in the same column, eg a Queen and a 2, or a 9 and a 5, appearing together in a column. This is likely to happen on average in about four columns per deal. The player must note these occurrences and take the earliest opportunity to play one of the cards of the pair, since to leave, for example, a Queen and a 2 in the same column when the other three pairs of Queens and 2s have been discarded clearly leads to failure.

Friday the Thirteenth

When the thirteenth of a month falls on a Friday, it is reckoned to be an unlucky day. Quite why this interesting little patience game has been saddled with this name remains a mystery however. It is a simple and unusual game with an attractive outcome when successful.

Alternative names	None
Number of packs required	One
Time needed to get it out	Four minutes
Prospects of success	About nine in ten

Aim
To end with 13 piles of four cards, each pile being in ascending sequence of four with the top cards ranging from Ace on the left to King on the right.

Preparation
Four cards, a Jack, Queen, King and Ace of any suits, are ranged in a row with spaces for nine more cards to range to the right, as shown in the illustration overleaf. These 13 cards will be foundation cards.

Play
The remaining 48 cards are turned over one at a time and built if possible in ascending sequence onto the foundation cards, eg Queen on Jack, King on Queen, Ace on King, 2 on Ace and so on. The foundation space to the right of the Ace is filled with a 2, the space to its right a 3, and so on until the 13th foundation card in the tableau will be a 10. The foundation cards must be played in the right order, eg the 2 foundation must be in place before the 3 foundation can be played, and so on.

If a card cannot be played immediately, it is played face up to a waste heap. The top card of the waste heap is always available for play.

When the stock is exhausted, the waste heap is turned over and, without being shuffled, is played card by card again. There is no further redeal. Each pile is built up to four cards only, resulting in the attractive finish with the piles topped by Ace (at the far left) to King (at the far right).

Strategy It is usually best, when there is a choice to establish a new foundation card or to build onto an existing pile, to establish the new foundation card. If a card is turned up which can be played to one of two piles, one of which it will complete, it is often better to play it to the other pile, therefore leaving both piles incomplete and thus giving an extra chance for the next turned-up card to be playable to a pile.

Friday the Thirteenth

Example game

The illustration shows four cards laid out at the beginning of the game, forming the first of the foundations. As the cards are dealt, the only ranks which can be played at the moment are Queen (on the Jack), King (on the Queen), Ace (on the King) and 2, which can be played onto the Ace or, preferably, onto the space in the tableau to the right of the Ace. Once a 2 is in place, a 3 can be played next to it and so on, until the

last tableau space is filled with a 10. Once the initial cards are in place they can be regarded as foundation cards, on which three more cards are built in sequence, regardless of suit. A successful game will therefore end with the first pile headed by an Ace, the next by a 2, and so on up to the King at the end.

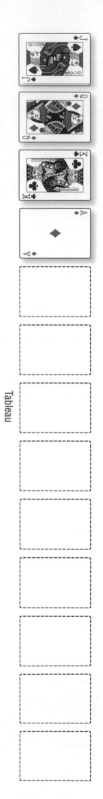

Tableau

Frog

Frog is a simple game requiring little thought, but judgement is needed when deciding upon which waste heap to place the numerous unplayable cards.

Alternative names	Toad, Toad-in-the-Hole
Number of packs required	Two
Time needed to get it out	15 minutes
Prospects of success	About one in six

Aim
To end with eight piles of 13 cards in sequence from Ace to King, the sequences being irrespective of suit or colour.

Preparation
The two packs are thoroughly shuffled, and a row of 13 overlapping cards is dealt as a reserve. Some players are happy for the reserve to be merely a pile, but it makes the game more interesting if the player can see which cards are becoming available as the game progresses. If any Aces are dealt among the 13, they are extracted to begin a row of Aces beneath the reserve. The reserve is then made up to 13 cards. The Aces are foundations and all eight are placed in a row as they become available during the game. If none is dealt in the reserve, the player is allowed to extract an Ace from the pack as his first foundation card.

Play
The cards are dealt one at a time, with Aces placed as they become available in the foundation row, and being built upon up to Kings, irrespective of suit and colour. The fully exposed card at the end of the reserve is available for play, and should be built upon a foundation as soon as possible. This releases the next card for play. When a card turned from the stock cannot be built to a foundation, it is played to one of five waste heaps, the top cards of which are always available for play. It is more interesting if the waste heaps, like the reserve, are overlapped so that the player can plan his play when he has a choice. There is no redeal.

Strategy It is wise to reserve one of the waste heaps for Kings and Queens, as they are the last cards to be played to a foundation and will block the game if scattered around the waste heaps. Where possible, build down upon the waste heaps, trying to build descending sequences that can be played off to a foundation one after the other when the opportunity arises.

Example game

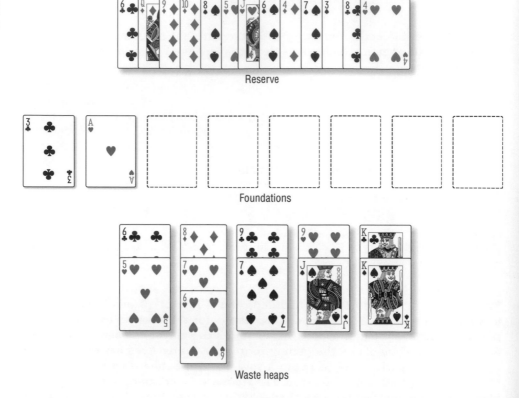

Reserve

Foundations

Waste heaps

The game has just begun. Two Aces have been played to foundations, and the first has just been built up to the ♣3. The ♥4 at the end of the reserve can now be played to it, with a choice of following plays, including building the ♥5, ♥6 and ♠7 from the first three waste heaps, thus enabling the ♣8 to be built on the foundation from the reserve, followed by the ♣9 to empty a waste heap. Five waste heaps have been begun, with Kings already played to the fifth one. The ♠J has unfortunately had to be piled on top of a 9 on one waste heap, but it is early days.

Gargantua

Players of Klondike (see p71), one of the most popular of all one-pack patience games, will enjoy Gargantua, the double-pack version, although they will find it is much easier to get out.

Alternative names	Double Klondike, Harp
Number of packs required	Two
Time needed to get it out	20 minutes
Prospects of success	About one in three

Aim
To finish with eight piles, two for each suit, with the suits being built in ascending sequence from Ace to King.

Preparation
The two packs are shuffled together thoroughly and a row of nine cards is dealt, the first face up and the remainder face down. Beginning with the second card in the row, another eight cards are dealt on top of, and overlapping, the first row, with the first face up and the remainder face down. Rows continue to be laid out in this manner, reducing the number of cards by one each time, and dealing the first face up, until the tableau is completed as illustrated overleaf.

Space for eight foundation cards is left along the top of the tableau. As available, the Aces will be played here, and the object is to build on them in ascending suit sequence to the Kings.

Play
The cards available for play are the nine face-up cards, one at the foot of each column. Available Aces are played immediately to a foundation row, and are built on as eligible cards become free. Available cards may also be packed on each other in descending order and alternate colours. Groups of cards in sequence can be played as a whole unit from one column to another provided they maintain a correct sequence with the card they are played onto. When a column becomes empty by virtue of all its cards being played elsewhere, the space is filled by an available King or sequence headed by a King. If the space cannot be filled from elsewhere in the tableau, it must remain empty until a King is turned over from the stock. When all available moves have been made in the initial tableau, the remaining cards, the stock, are taken face down in hand and dealt one at a time to a waste heap. The top card of the waste heap is always available for play.

When the stock is exhausted, the waste heap may be turned over without shuffling and redealt once only.

Gargantua

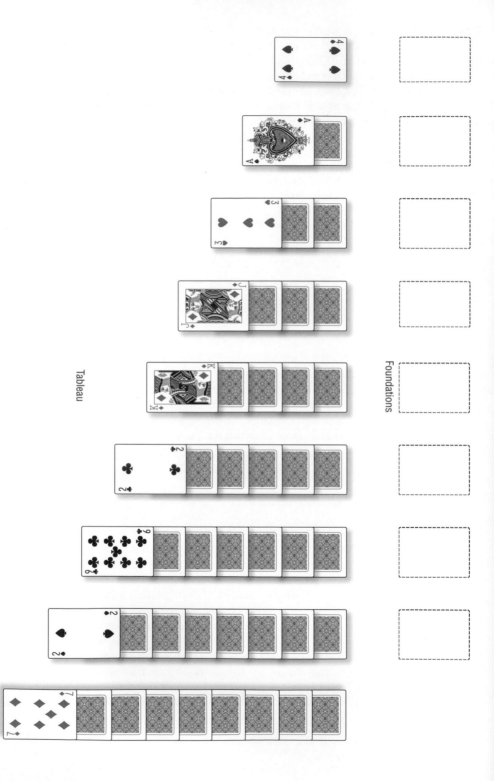

Tableau

Foundations

Strategy This is one of those attractive games that can pleasantly surprise by coming out with a rush at the end. Although not always possible, it pays to try to keep the foundations built up evenly. The writer once got this patience out after having turned over the last card in the redeal with four cards in the waste heap, no foundations built above 10, and three cards still face down in the tableau, including an Ace. Luckily the last card turned over proved playable, the game continued, all cards became exposed (the Ace was the last of the 104) and the game succeeded.

Example game
In the illustration, the ♠A is played to a foundation, and the ♠2 built upon it. The ♥3 is packed on ♠4, followed by ♣2. The four face-down cards exposed by the play of these four cards are turned over and become available themselves for play. When no other plays are possible, the top card is turned from the stock.

Gate

Gate is so-called because its tableau resembles a gate with posts and rails. It is an attractive game that is easy to get out. A simple change to the rules gives a variant (mentioned at the end of this description), which makes the game much harder.

Alternative names	None
Number of packs required	One
Time needed to get it out	Six minutes
Prospects of success	About five in six

Aim
To finish with the four suits in separate piles arranged in sequence from Ace up to King.

Preparation
Five cards are dealt face up in a column to the left of the tableau, and five face up in a column to the right, with space for two rows of four face-up cards to be dealt between them. The two columns represent gate posts and the cards in them are reserves. Between them the two rows of four cards represent the two lower rails of the gate. The top rail of the gate is not dealt, and is reserved for the foundation cards (see illustration).

Play
The cards available for play are those forming the rails of the gate, and the bottom cards of each of the gate posts.

Any available Ace is immediately played to a foundation space, where it is built on in ascending order of rank as the respective cards become available.

Cards in the rails can also be built upon in descending sequence of alternate colours, either singly or as a sequence. A space occurring in the rails is filled by a card from the foot of either of the posts. When a card is played from a post, the card above it becomes available for filling gaps in the rails. Cards removed from the posts are not replaced. When the posts have disappeared, which usually happens quickly, a space in the rails is filled immediately by the top card of the waste heap.

The cards from the stock are turned over one at a time and played if possible to a foundation or the rails. Unplayable cards are played to a single waste heap, the top card of which is always available for play. The waste heap is not redealt.

The game is one of those where the waste heap often builds up quickly and unpromisingly, but evaporates just as quickly as the Aces appear.

Example game

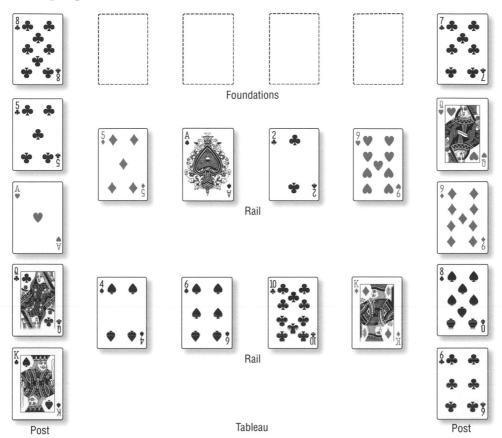

Foundations

Rail

Rail

Post   Tableau   Post

The cards were dealt to the tableau as illustrated. The ♠A is played to the foundation row (the ♥A cannot yet be played as it is not at the foot of the left-hand post). The ♥9 is played to ♣10, ♦5 to ♠6, ♠4 to ♦5, leaving four spaces in the rails. The ♠K and ♣Q are played to the rails (the ♣Q is built straight onto ♦K). This releases the ♥A to its foundation. The ♣6 and ♠8 are played to the rails, the ♠8 being played straight to ♥9. The ♦9 is played to the rails, which allows the ♥Q to be played straight to the ♠K. There is still a space in the rails, and the ♣5 is played to it allowing the ♣8 to be played to the ♦9.

That is all the building that can be done immediately. There is only one card left in the posts.

The first card is now turned over from the stock, and is played to a foundation, the rails or to begin the waste heap, and so on.

Variant
Since a patience game that nearly always comes out can be as boring as one which hardly ever does, some players prefer a version of the game that is harder than the one described. This is achieved by allowing building in the tableau only with single cards, ie one cannot move a sequence from one pile to

another. This greatly restricts the number of moves possible and makes for a more difficult game (with a success rate of only about one in 25). A player who plays this version with more and more annoyance can release his frustration by ending the session in getting out the easier version.

Grandfather's Clock

Grandfather's Clock is a better patience game than Clock (see p33), in that it rewards judgement, and an experienced player will get it out more often than not. However, by the time children can play it well they can already tell the time, so Clock has its place for them.

Alternative names	None
Number of packs required	One
Time needed to get it out	Eight minutes
Prospects of success	Two in three

Aim

To build a clockface, using all 52 cards, with twelve piles, each headed by a card appropriate to its place on the face (Ace representing one, Jack 11 and Queen 12, and ordinary cards their pip number).

Preparation

Twelve cards are removed from the pack: ♥2, 6, 10; ♠3, 7, Jack; ♦4, 8, Queen; and ♣5, 9, King. They are arranged to form a clockface, with the ♣9 at 12 o'clock, and the others arranged in a circle in the positions shown in the illustration overleaf. The remaining 40 cards are shuffled and dealt below the clockface in five overlapping rows of eight cards each, as also shown.

Play

The object is to build up each of the cards in the clockface, in suit sequence, as far as its position on the dial requires. For example, ♣9 is built to ♣Q, representing 12 o'clock, ♥10 up to ♥A, representing one o'clock, and so on all round the face. The sequence of building is 'round the corner', ie Ace follows King and precedes 2. Thus the ♠J is built up with ♠Q, K, A, 2 to represent 2 o'clock. The ♥10, ♠J, ♦Q and ♣K foundations will require four cards, the others three.

The cards available for play are those at the foot of the eight columns. As well as being built to the foundations, ie the clockface, they can be packed upon each other in descending round-the-corner sequence regardless of suit, but only one card at a time. A sequence cannot be moved from one column to another as a unit. When a space appears because all the cards in a column have been played, it is filled by any single available card from another column.

The game is successful if all cards from the columns can be played to the clockface, which will end with each card on the face showing the correctly placed number.

Example game

The clockface foundations are laid and the cards dealt as in the illustration. The ♥7 followed by the ♥8, ♠Q and ♦K can be played directly to the foundations. This releases the ♥3 to the foundation. By packing ♣8 on ♠9, the ♥4 can be released to its foundation, and ♠10 to ♣J will release ♥5 to its foundation. This card represents 5 o'clock and building on that foundation is finished. Now ♠K can be packed on ♥A, ♣Q to ♠K, and ♦A and ♣10 are released to their foundations. And so on.

Herringbone

Herringbone is a very attractive patience game for those who like elaborate layouts. Unfortunately, a long table (not to mention long arms) or two special patience packs of miniature cards are required. Otherwise one can use the alternative layout given under Variant, below.

Alternative names	None
Number of packs required	Two
Time needed to get it out	15 minutes
Prospects of success	About three in four

Aim
To finish with a line of eight piles, two for each suit, all built down in suit sequence from Jack to Ace, with the Kings and Queens protruding at an angle on each side of the piles, making an overall pattern of a herringbone.

Preparation
The packs are shuffled together and two rows of three cards are dealt face up. This forms the tableau.

Play
As they become available, the eight Jacks are placed in a long, upright, non-overlapping line to be foundations. On these are built cards in suit sequence from 10 down to Ace.

All the cards in the tableau, plus the top card of a waste heap, are available for play.

As well as being built to foundations, cards in the tableau can be packed on each other in suit sequences of *ascending* order of rank (not descending, as in nearly all other games). Sequences can be packed as a whole unit onto another tableau card, providing the suit sequence is preserved from one pile to the other. Eventually, when the opportunity arises, sequences are built one card at a time onto the foundation.

After the initial deal, when any Jacks have been removed to a foundation, and any packing on the tableau has been completed, the stock is turned over one card at a time, and each card played either to the foundations or the tableau, or to a single waste heap. When a space appears in the tableau it is filled by the top card of the waste heap, or if no waste heap yet exists the next card of the stock.

When Kings and Queens become available, they are discarded one each beneath the Jack of the suit in the foundation, protruding at an angle to each side to form the herringbone pattern which gives the game its name. They do not have to be played at the same time, but they cannot be played there until the Jack is in place. If it isn't, they must remain in the tableau or in the waste heap, waiting their turn. Note that tableau piles cannot be built beyond 10, as the Jacks go straight to the foundations.

Do not despair when vital cards get buried in the waste heap. When the stock is exhausted one redeal is allowed, and it is surprising how quickly the cards vanish onto the foundations. To form the new stock, the waste heap is turned over without shuffling.

Example game
The illustration shows a game in progress. Four Jacks are in place as foundations: ♣J, ♦J, ♠J, and the second ♦J. The ♣J has already been built down to ♣9. Some Kings and Queens are already in place. The ♥Q has been in the tableau since the initial deal, awaiting a ♥J to become available. The card just turned from the stock is an ♣8, which can be played to the foundation, with ♣7, 6, 5, 4 following it from the tableau, and the space filled by ♥2 from the waste heap.

Variant
A more manageable layout is to line up the six tableau cards in a row, and play the Jacks as they become available into a row above them, discarding one King and one Queen above each when appropriate. But then that would not be Herringbone patience...

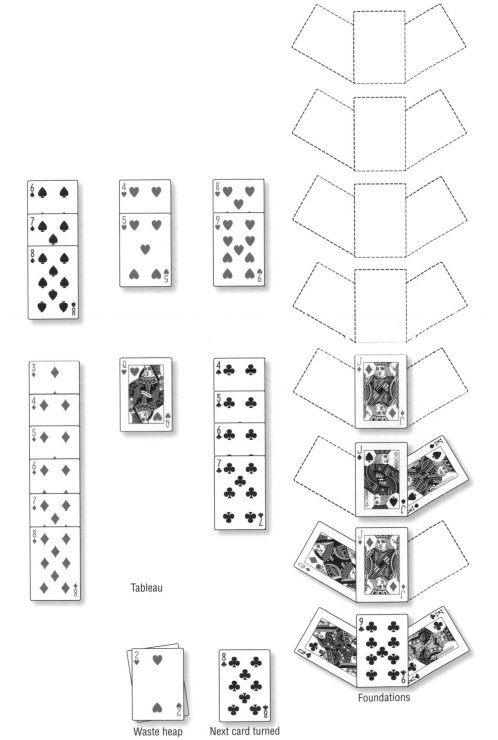

Tableau

Foundations

Waste heap   Next card turned

King Albert

This game is believed to be named after King Albert I of Belgium. In 1948 it was described by Basil Dalton, the distinguished writer on card games, as 'quite the best single-pack game of patience ever invented'.

King Albert rewards intelligent play, which makes a mystery of its alternative name, Idiot's Delight, although this name has been given to other patience games as well.

Alternative names	Idiot's Delight
Number of packs required	One
Time needed to get it out	15 minutes
Prospects of success	About two in five

Aim

To end with four piles of cards, one for each suit, in sequence from Ace up to King.

Preparation

A row of nine cards is dealt face up to the table. A second face-up row of eight is dealt to the first eight cards, overlapping them. Further face-up rows are then dealt, of seven cards down to one, as shown in the illustration opposite.

The seven remaining cards, the reserve, are laid face up in a row by the side. The four blank spaces are the foundations where the Aces will go when they become available.

Play

The cards available for play are the cards exposed at the base of each column, and the cards in the reserve. When available, Aces are played to a space in the foundation row, where they are built on in sequence in their suits up to the Kings. An available card, as well as being played to a foundation of its own suit in ascending sequence, may be packed on to an exposed card at the bottom of a column in descending sequence of alternate colours.

If a column becomes vacant, it may be filled by any exposed card.

Cards may be moved one at a time only; in other words, a sequence cannot be moved from one column to another as in many similar patience games.

Example game

In the layout opposite, the ♦A and ♥A can be played immediately to their foundations. The ♥2 can be played from the reserve to the foundation. The ♣2 can be packed on the ♦3, which empties a column, to which can be played the ♠K. This releases the ♣A to its foundation, and the ♣2 can be built on it. The

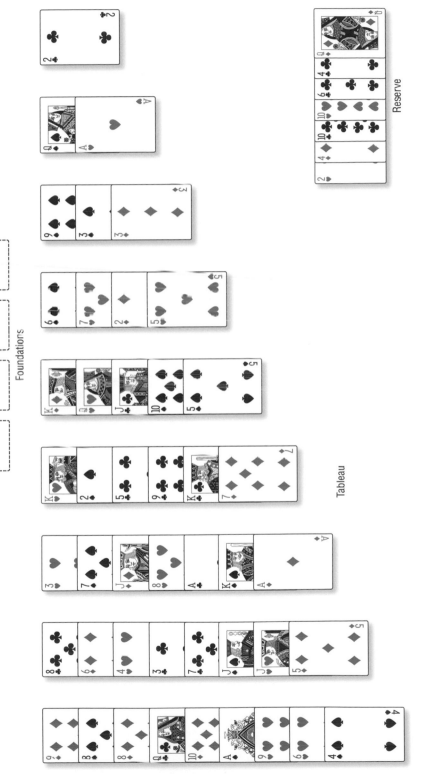

Reserve

Foundations

Tableau

♣6 from the reserve can be packed on ♦7 and ♦5 packed on it. The ♥J can be played to ♠Q. The ♦Q can be packed on ♠K and ♠J packed on it. The ♠4 can be packed on ♦5 and the ♥6 on ♣7. The ♣10 can be packed on ♥J and ♥9 packed on it, releasing ♠A to its foundation, and so on.

This example appears hardly likely to go much further: the positions of the ♠2 and ♥3 are likely to block the building on these foundations for too long, especially as the ♣K is blocking the way to the ♠2. However, with care it can be played out.

Klondike

Klondike is a widely played patience game, perhaps the most widely played of all. It is often misnamed Canfield, which is really the name by which Demon is known in the USA, or sometimes simply Patience.

Alternative names	Canfield (mistakenly), Fascination, Triangle
Number of packs required	One
Time needed to get it out	Ten minutes
Prospects of success	About 1 in 30

Aim
To end with four piles of cards, one for each suit, in sequence from Ace up to King.

Preparation
The cards are shuffled and seven cards are dealt face down in a row. Six face-down cards are then dealt in a row underneath but one card to the right, each overlapping a card in the row above. Further rows, each shorter than the previous, are added until the tableau is completed, and the first card in each row is turned face up, as shown in the illustration overleaf. The four blank spaces are the foundations where the Aces will go when they become available. The cards not dealt form the stock.

Play
The cards available for play are those exposed at the foot of each of the columns, and they can be built to a foundation, or can be packed on each other in descending sequences of alternate colours. Cards can be packed from one column to another in units, for example a ◆7, ♣6 exposed at the foot of a column can be transferred as a whole to a ♣8 or ♠8 exposed at the foot of another column. Aces should be played to the foundations as soon as they become available.

When a card or group of cards is transferred from a column, the bottom card of the column is turned over and becomes available. If a column is emptied, it can be filled only by an available King, either with other cards attached to it in sequence, or alone.

When all the cards in the tableau have been played as far as possible, the stock is taken into the hand, and the top card is turned over and is available for play. If it cannot be played to the tableau or the foundations it is placed face up on the table to begin a waste-pile, or 'talon'. The card at the top of the talon is always available for play.

If the turned-over stock card can be played, all other moves which then become possible in the tableau can be made, including those resulting from the exposure of new cards at the foot of the columns. When all possible moves have been made, the next card is turned over from the stock to the talon, and so on.

It is not obligatory to play a card to its foundation immediately, but once it is built there it cannot be moved back into the tableau. The stock is turned over once only, ie there is no redeal. The game is won if all the foundations are built up to the Kings.

Example game

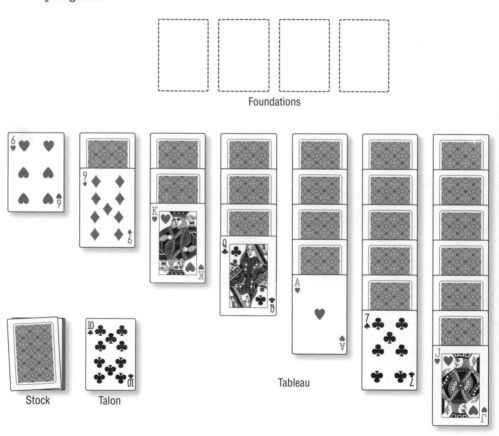

Foundations

Stock   Talon

Tableau

In the illustration, the ♥A is moved to a foundation, and the card below it faced; the ♥6 is packed on the ♣7; the ♥K is moved to fill the column from which the ♥6 was taken; the ♣Q is packed on the ♥K, followed by the ♥J; with each time the face-down card which finds itself at the foot of a column turned face up.

The first card turned from stock to begin the talon is the ♣10, but this can immediately be packed on ♥J, and the ♦9 can then be packed on to it.

La Belle Lucie

La Belle Lucie, with its charming name (perhaps the French know who La Belle Lucie was) is a classic patience game with a pleasing layout. All the cards are laid out at the beginning, so there is plenty of opportunity for skill. It nevertheless remains a difficult game to get out.

Alternative names	Alexander the Great, Clover Leaf, Fan, Midnight Oil
Number of packs required	One
Time needed to get it out	20 minutes
Prospect of success	About one in twelve

Aim
To end with four piles of cards, one for each suit, in sequence from Ace up to King.

Preparation
The cards are dealt in 17 fans of three cards each, with one odd card, spread out on the playing surface. Traditionally the fans are themselves arranged in the shape of a fan, but this requires a very large table.

Play
The top (ie the right-hand) card of each fan, plus the odd card, are available for play. As Aces become available they are placed below the tableau as foundations, and other available cards are built upon them in ascending suit sequence. Available cards can also be packed onto each other in descending suit sequence, one at a time; once a card has another packed onto it, the sequence cannot then be moved elsewhere. If all cards in a fan are played, the fan is not replaced.

When all possible moves have been made, all the cards not built on a foundation may be picked up, shuffled, and redealt in fans of three. The last fan might consist of only one or two cards. Further moves are made until no more are possible, when the cards remaining in the tableau can again be picked up, shuffled and redealt as before.

Two redeals only are allowed, and the game is lost if, after the second redeal, it is impossible to build all the cards to the foundations.

Strategy Be careful when choosing where to play cards to fans, as the wrong choice can block play entirely in a situation in which an alternative could allow many more moves. This is especially important after the second redeal as a block now will end the game.

Example game

Tableau of fans

Foundations

In the layout shown above, ♣A and ♣2 can be played to a foundation; ♣8 can be packed on ♣9; ♣7 on ♣8; ♥3 on ♥4. This allows both ♥A and ♠A to be played to their foundations. It is important now to pack ♥9 on ♥10 before ♥8 on ♥9, which would block the ♦A. By looking ahead, one can see how the 5s of all four suits can, with careful play, become very useful. The ♥9 is therefore packed on ♥10, allowing ♦A to be played to its foundation; ♥8 is packed on ♥9, ♦5 packed on ♦6; ♦4 on ♦5; ♦2 to foundation; ♣4 to ♣5; ♠3 to ♠4; ♠5 to ♠6; ♦8 to ♦9. The

♠2 is released to its foundation, which allows all the spades up to ♠7 to follow. Now the hearts up to ♥6 can be played to their foundation. The clubs up to ♣5 can follow. More thought is now necessary. Packing the ♠9 onto ♠10 to get at ♣6 would be a mistake, because it blocks ♠8. First it is ♠10 to ♠J; now ♠9 to ♠10. This releases the whole of the club suit to the foundation.

And so on. This game will be got out in one deal, an extremely rare occurrence. But one mistake with ♥8 early on would have ended the play on the first deal there and then, necessitating a second deal with only limited progress made. An excellent patience game.

Lady of the Manor

This is a simple game, which has an attractive and unusual tableau. It can be played in a casual manner, since luck plays a large part in getting it out, but thoughtful play can improve a player's chances of success.

Alternative names	None
Number of packs required	Two
Time needed to get it out	15 minutes
Prospects of success	About 1 in 15

Aim
To finish with eight piles built from Aces to Kings of any suit or colour.

Preparation
The eight Aces are removed from the two packs. The packs are then well shuffled. Just over half the combined pack is taken in hand face down, and a row of four cards is dealt face up to the table. Continue dealing cards to these four until there are four piles of twelve cards each. The remainder of the pack is then sorted into ranks, and a crescent of twelve face-up piles is arranged above the four dealt piles, from the 2s on the left to the Kings (see illustration). The piles in the crescent will contain differing numbers of cards, and it is possible, but rare, that a rank will not be represented in the crescent, in which case a space is left. If this happens, the game is extremely unlikely to be successful. This is the tableau. The eight Aces are then set out in a row, in any order, below the four dealt piles. These Aces are the foundations.

Play
The top cards of all piles in the tableau, ie both the row of four cards and the sorted cards in the crescent are available to build on the foundations. The foundations can be built on in any order, and several may be being built on simultaneously. The only rule governing play is that when a card from the row of four is available it must be played before a card from the crescent. This does not hinder the player, because the game cannot be won until each card in the four piles is built. If the game comes to a halt before all the cards in the four piles have been built to the foundations, the game is lost.

Example game
The tableau of four piles of twelve cards has been dealt, and the remaining cards have been sorted into ranks and laid out in a crescent. The eight Aces are in a row to form the foundations. The ♦2 must be played to a foundation, and the player would be advised to build the foundation up to 5 from the crescent in order to play the ♣6 and ♠7 upon it. By then three new cards will be exposed, and the player should base his strategy on what these cards are.

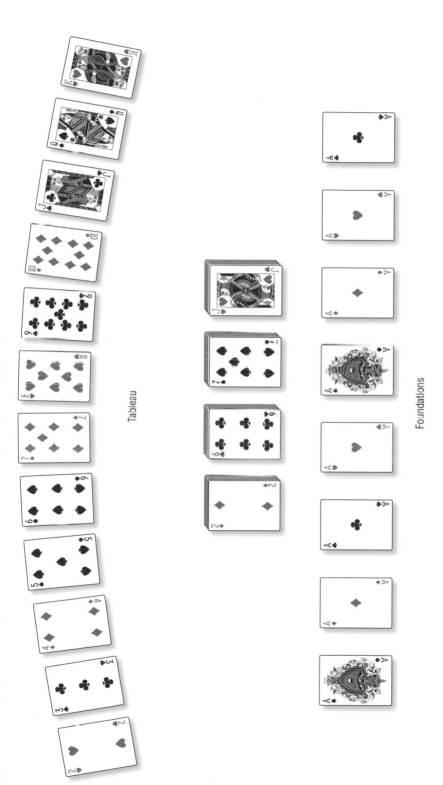

Tableau

Foundations

Strategy The game is lost when a card gets buried below a higher card in one of the piles. So when dealing the piles, note any with a low card, say 2, 3 or 4 at or near the bottom of a pile, and when choices of play arise choose the card in that pile. Note which ranks of cards in the crescent are running low and try to build on foundations which do not need those ranks. Do not be in a hurry to build high cards like Queens and Kings from the crescent to the foundations, but instead try to develop as many other foundations by playing cards from the row of four piles. In this way you might expose a King, say, which you could play to a foundation, whereas had you played a King earlier from the crescent, you would be unable to, and the King would remain blocking one of the four piles.

Lady Palk

Lady Palk is an old and popular patience game, so old that nobody seems to know who Lady Palk was. It is very difficult to get out and requires concentration, since the player is often provided with many options for play.

Alternative names	None
Number of packs required	Two
Time needed to get it out	30 minutes
Prospects of success	About 1 in 20

Aim

To end with two columns of four piles, each pile built up from Ace to King in ascending suit sequence.

Preparation

The two packs are thoroughly shuffled together. Sixteen cards are then dealt face up to the left of the tableau in four rows of four, followed by a similar four rows of four to the right of the tableau, with a space between the two blocks of 16 cards for two columns of four cards each. The two blocks of 16 cards are known as the left wing and the right wing. The space is for the foundation cards (see illustration).

Play

The eight outside cards in the tableau, ie the four cards on the extreme left of the left wing, and those on the extreme right of the right wing, are available to play. When one is played, the card inside it becomes the outside card. Aces, when available, are played to a foundation pile, and available cards can then be built upon them in ascending sequences of suit up to the King.

As well as being built on foundations, available cards can be packed on each other in descending order of rank irrespective of suit and colour. Sequences and part-sequences can be moved as a whole to another exposed card, provided that a proper sequence is maintained. In this game packing in the tableau will necessarily be sideways, rather than the usual downwards. When a space occurs in the tableau by virtue of a row of four cards in either wing having been played, the space may be filled by playing an exposed King, or a sequence headed by a King, into it. If no such is available, the space must remain until a King does become available.

Once all moves have been made on the original layout, the stock is turned over one at a time from hand, and the card turned is played to a foundation or to the tableau, or if neither is possible, to a single waste heap. The top card of the waste heap is always available for play.

There is no redeal, but there is one unusual privilege given to the player which is not allowed in almost all other patience games of this type: a player may play a card, or a succession of cards back from a foundation to the tableau, provided the proper sequence is maintained. This is called 'worrying back', and it allows the player to manoeuvre cards around at will, so long as the rules of the sequences are obeyed.

Example game

♠9 is played to ♠10, ♦A is played to its foundation, ♣Q is played to ♥K, ♦J is played to ♣Q, the two ♣As are played to foundations, ♠5 is played to ♠6 (bottom right), and the sequence ♥K, ♣Q and ♦J can be moved to fill the space on the right wing created by moving ♠5.

Further moves can be made before the first card of the stock needs to be turned; this particular game has begun well.

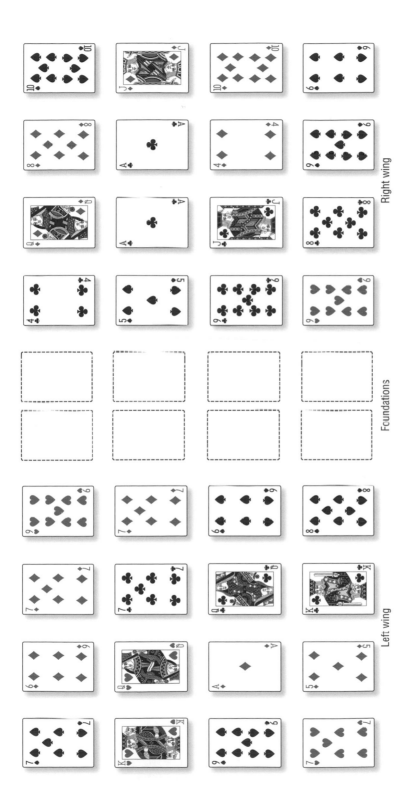

Right wing

Foundations

Left wing

Le Cadran

Le Cadran is an old and popular patience game, usually included in books under the name Napoleon at St Helena, it being one of those games said to have amused Napoleon during his exile on the island. This book prefers to honour a different strand of history by calling it Le Cadran, this being the name under which it was described in the first collection of patience games published in English, by Lady Adelaide Cadogan around 1870.

Alternative names	Big Forty, Forty Thieves, Napoleon at St Helena
Number of packs required	Two
Time needed to get it out	20 minutes
Prospects of success	About 1 in 20

Aim

To finish with eight piles of cards, each built up in sequence from Ace to King in a single suit.

Preparation

The two packs are well shuffled together. Forty cards are then dealt in ten columns of four, the cards in each column overlapping each other. Room should be left for a row of eight cards above the tableau, this being for the foundation cards, which are the Aces (see illustration).

Play

The top cards of the tableau piles, ie those at the foot of the columns, are available for play. They can be built on in ascending suit sequence to the Aces, which are played to the foundation row as they become available, or they can be packed upon each other in descending suit sequence, but only one card at a time (ie two or more cards forming a sequence cannot be moved as a unit from one tableau column to another).

The stock is dealt one card at a time to a waste heap, the top card of which is always available for play. When a tableau column is emptied, all its cards having been played, the space is filled by any available card from another column or the waste heap.

Example game

The cards are dealt as in the illustration. The ♠A is played to a foundation, ♠9 is played to ♠10, allowing ♠2 and ♠3 to be played to the foundation, ♣10 played to ♣J, ♦J played to ♦Q, ♣6 to ♣7, ♣K to the space, ♠4 to the foundation, ♦A to the foundation, followed by ♦2, ♥A to the foundation, ♠8 to ♠9, ♣Q to ♣K, ♥2 to the foundation, ♥J to a space, ♥3 to the foundation, ♥10 (column 6) to ♥J, ♦Q to the remaining space. Now the first card is turned from the stock.

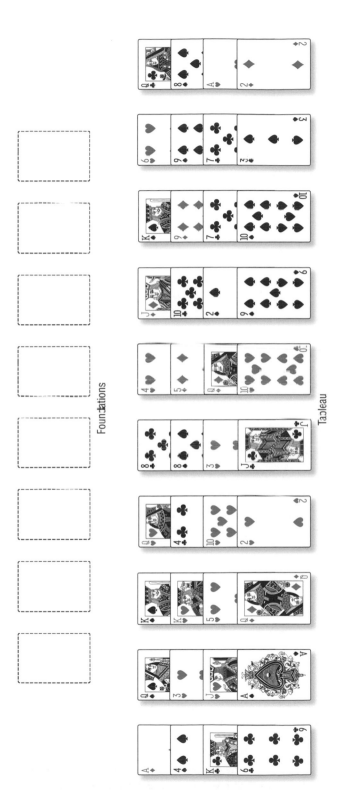

Foundations

Tableau

Strategy The severe restrictions on how cards can be moved make this a difficult patience game to get out and the player's best chance lies in being able to manipulate the columns in the tableau by trying to create spaces to which cards blocking progress can be played. Since cards can be transferred from one column to another only singly, it might sometimes be better not to pack cards on others each time an opportunity occurs.

Variant

To make the game slightly less difficult, some players allow the stock to be played face up, so that when the player takes the top card of the stock to play, he can see the card that follows, and can base his choice of play on this extra knowledge.

Legitimist

The supporters of the legitimate claim of members of the house of Bourbon to the French throne are said to give this patience game its name. It is not a game of much skill. Its attraction is that it usually comes very close to success, and the player's interest is held right to the end. It is similar to, but more difficult than, the one-pack Friday the Thirteenth (see p53).

Alternative names	None
Number of packs required	Two
Time needed to get it out	Twelve minutes
Prospects of success	About one in five

Aim
To finish with eight piles of 13 cards, all built in descending sequence irrespective of suit and colour and headed, from the left, by Ace, King, Queen, Jack, 10, 9, 8, and 7.

Preparation
Any King is extracted and laid to the left of the tableau as the first in what will be a row of eight foundation cards. The two packs of cards are thoroughly shuffled together and taken face down in the hand for dealing. It is easier if half the pack is put aside for the time being, as 103 cards are difficult to hold at once.

Play
The cards are turned one by one to a waste heap, the top of which is always available. As they appear a Queen, a Jack, a 10, a 9, an 8, a 7 and a 6 are played alongside the King on the table to be foundation cards. They must be played to the table only in that order, eg the Jack foundation cannot be played until the Queen is in place. The first card to be played to the table is therefore always a Queen.

As soon as a foundation card is played to the table it can be built upon in descending order, irrespective of a colour or suit, whenever appropriate cards become available. The sequence is 'round the corner', ie King follows Ace.

The foundation cards are built on until they support a pile of 13 cards, ie the King is built down to the Ace, Queen to King, Jack to Queen, 10 to Jack, 9 to 10, 8 to 9, 7 to 8 and 6 to 7.

When all the stock has been dealt, the waste heap is turned over without shuffling, and dealt again. A third deal is allowed, and the game is won if at the end of it all eight foundation piles are built down to Ace, King, Queen, Jack, 10, 9, 8 and 7 respectively. If not, the game is lost.

Strategy The best chance of getting out the patience is to overcome the temptation to build down a foundation as soon as the opportunity arises. The objective should be to build upon each foundation as evenly as possible, and refrain from completing them as much as one can. This does not mean playing to the waste heap a card which can be played to a foundation, but that when a card can be played to two, three or four foundations, as often occurs, the foundation which is least built upon should be chosen. This ensures that towards the end there are still eight piles upon which the card turned from the stock might fit. Each time a foundation is completed, the chance of the next card from the stock being playable is reduced. This can be vital when only two or three foundations are left to be completed.

Limited

Limited is not a particularly well-known patience game, but it can be a very satisfactory one, in that it sometimes produces runs of success which enable it to be got out from what appear to be hopeless positions. It is similar to Le Cadran (see p82) and may have been derived from it, but as there are more options for the player it is a better game.

Alternative names	None
Number of packs required	Two
Time needed to get it out	20 minutes
Prospects of success	About one in five

Aim
To end with eight piles of cards, two for each suit, in sequence from Ace up to King.

Preparation
The two packs of cards are shuffled together making a pack of 104 cards. Three rows of twelve cards are then dealt, face up, forming the tableau.

Play
The cards in the bottom row are available for play. Any Aces in the bottom row are immediately played to a new row above the tableau, forming the foundations, where they can be built upon in ascending suit sequences. When a card is taken from the bottom row, the card in the middle row above it becomes available for play, and when that is played, the card above in the top row is available.

Available cards can also be packed upon each other in descending suit sequence. The card moved should be overlapped onto the other, to establish that the two are a pair. A pair cannot be moved again or have a third card packed upon it: it must remain where it is until the cards can be played to a foundation (it is not compulsory to play the two cards to a foundation together – for tactical reasons it might be preferable to play one but not the other, in which case the card remaining in the tableau ceases to be part of a pair). It is not compulsory to pack on other cards, and it may be advisable not to.

It will be clear why the game is called Limited – the moves are very limited.

The remaining cards are the stock. Once all initial moves have been made, the stock is turned over one card at a time. In practice, as the stock is of 68 cards, it is usual to put half aside, while taking the other half face down in hand and turning them one at a time face up to the table. If a card can be played to a foundation or packed on an available card, it can be, but the latter is not compulsory. If a card turned over from the stock is played to a foundation, all subsequent desirable moves in the tableau can be made before the next card is turned over from the stock. A card that is not played to the tableau or a foundation is played face up to a waste heap. The card on top of the waste heap is always available for play.

If a column in the tableau is emptied, it is replaced by any available card, ie by a card from the top of the waste heap or from the bottom row of the tableau. Vacancies need not be filled immediately, and it usually pays to wait for a suitable card to appear from the stock. A suitable card would be one which would enable a card from another column to be packed on it, thus releasing an Ace or other vital card which was blocked.

When the whole stock is exhausted, the player is allowed a second turn, though that itself is a limited one. In this, the waste pile is turned over and the first four cards are dealt in a line, face up, below the tableau. These are called 'grace cards', and are available to be played to a foundation, packed on a card at the foot of a column or used to fill a vacant column. If a card is played, it is replaced by the next card of the stock, so the grace cards remain at four.

If a stage is reached when no cards are playable, even the four grace cards, there is one last move. A fifth card is added to the grace cards from the stock. If that cannot be played, the game is lost. A fifth card can only be added once.

This game sounds almost impossible to get out, and newcomers to it will be convinced of this as the waste pile builds up alarmingly. But sudden turns of fortune occur, and once several Aces are released to foundations it speeds up.

Example game

In the tableau illustrated opposite, the ♦A and ♥A can be played to foundations, and the ♥2 can follow. The ♣5 can be packed on ♣6 and ♠2 on ♠3. Now the ♦10 can be packed on ♦J, releasing ♠A to a foundation. The ♠2, 3 can go to the foundation. The ♠6 (column 8) can be packed on ♠7, allowing ♦2 to be played to a foundation. With three foundations established and a vacant column, this is an excellent start.

You might now consider playing ♣Q to the vacant column, thus releasing ♦3 to a foundation and the ♥Q to the ♥K, or you may turn a card or two of the stock to see what might become available.

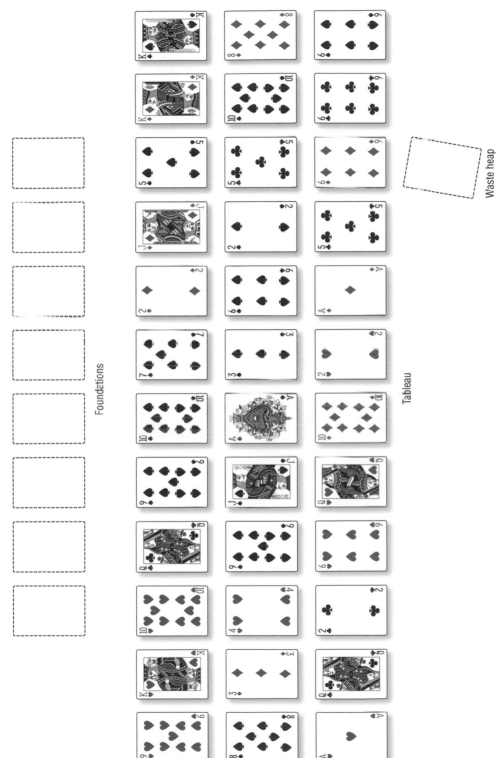

Foundations

Tableau

Waste heap

Little Spider

Little Spider is a game where luck plays a big part, but concentration can improve the chances of success, and the really skilful player should be able to get it out more often than not. The name is thought to come from the eight piles in the tableau, a spider having eight legs.

Alternative names	None
Number of packs required	One
Time needed to get it out	20 minutes
Prospects of success	One in two

Aim

To finish with two suits of the same colour built up in separate piles in sequence from Aces to Kings, and the two suits of the other colour each built down in descending sequence from Kings to Aces.

Preparation

After shuffling, eight cards are dealt in two rows of four, one above the other with a space between them for the row of four foundation cards, which will be placed there as they become available in play. The eight cards (they will later become piles) in the two rows form the tableau.

Play

If any of the cards dealt in the initial eight are Aces or Kings, they can be played to foundation spaces. The foundation cards are either two red Aces and two black Kings, or *vice versa*. The player may choose which.

The first foundation card to be put in place goes on the left-hand foundation space. If it is an Ace, the Ace of the same colour will go on the space next to it, with the remaining two spaces reserved for the Kings of the opposite colour. If it is a King, the opposite applies.

If none of the original eight cards is an Ace or King, then a further eight cards are dealt on top of them. The whole pack is dealt this way, with the last four cards going on the top row.

Between each deal of eight cards, available cards can be played to the centre. All the cards on the top of the eight piles are available, and if one is played, the card below it becomes available.

The chosen foundation cards (red Aces, black Kings or *vice versa*) in whichever row they are dealt, are played to the foundations as they appear and, during the deal, available cards can be built upon them in suit sequences (Aces up to Kings, Kings down to Aces) with the following restriction: while any available card in the top row can be played to its foundation, a card in the bottom row can only be played to its foundation if it is dealt directly below the foundation.

Once all the stock has been dealt, the rules change. Now available cards can be played to any foundation, no matter which row they are dealt to. Moreover, available cards can be packed, one at a time, onto other tableau cards in ascending or descending sequence irrespective of colour or rank. The sequence can change direction at will, and is 'round-the-corner', ie Ace comes between King and 2 in both directions. A space created by playing all the cards in a pile to the foundation or other piles is not filled.

The game is won if all foundations can be completely built on, from Ace to King or King to Ace and is lost if the piles become blocked and no further moves are possible.

Strategy The choice of which colour Aces and Kings to make foundations may depend upon which colour Ace or King is dealt first. However, players should note that if in the first eight cards dealt there is, say, a ♣Q and a ♦2, it would be best to choose red Kings and black Aces. If it were the other way round, once the ♣Q has been built on the ♣K foundation, and the ♦2 on the ♦A, those two piles disappear and the player has only six left with which to juggle the cards around.

It pays not to rush to build up the foundations, but to try to build up sequences in the tableau piles, ideally of the same suit, so that when the opportunity arises whole sequences can be skimmed off on to the foundation. The direction of the sequences in the piles should be the opposite to the direction of the cards on the foundation, although it is usually not too difficult to reverse a sequence on a tableau pile when necessary by playing the cards off individually onto another pile.

Example game
The illustration overleaf shows a game in progress during the initial dealing, ie before all the cards have been played to the tableau.

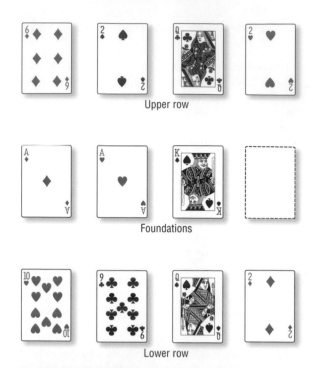

Upper row

Foundations

Lower row

The red Aces and black Kings have been chosen as foundations, and three of them are in position already. The ♣K has not yet appeared. The last eight cards to be dealt to the tableau provided the top cards as shown. The ♥2 can be built onto the ♥A foundation, because it is in the top row and available for all four foundations. The ♦2 cannot be built on ♦A, as it is in the bottom row and would need to be directly below the ♦A to be built there legitimately. The ♠Q can be built on the ♠K, however. Once these moves are made, eight more cards are dealt to the piles. Note the ♥10 cannot be packed on ♣9 in the tableau because all the cards are not yet dealt to the table.

Martha

Many patience games have been named after ladies of title. Martha, like the ever popular and equally mysterious Miss Milligan (see p98) are two ladies of less exalted rank who have been given this honour. Martha has a pleasing layout and most games are successful.

Alternative names	None
Number of packs required	One
Time needed to get it out	Eight minutes
Prospects of success	Nine in ten

Aim
To finish with four piles of cards, one for each suit, each pile running in sequence from Ace to King.

Preparation
The four Aces are removed from the pack and are placed in the centre of the table as foundation cards. The pack is then shuffled and a row of twelve face-down cards is dealt. Overlapping these, a row of twelve face-up cards, then another row face down and a final row face up are dealt, thus using up all the pack. This is the tableau (see illustration overleaf).

Play
The object is to play available cards on to the foundations in ascending suit sequence. The available cards are those at the foot of the twelve columns.

Any 2s in the initial deal are immediately played to their Aces. As a card is played, so the card replacing it at the foot of a column becomes available. If that card is face down, it is immediately turned face up.

As well as being played to foundations, available cards can be packed upon each other in descending sequence of alternating colour. A sequence can be moved from one column to another as a unit, provided it is in correct sequence with the card at the foot of the column to which it is moved. When a space appears by virtue of a whole column being emptied, it may be filled by a single available card from another column, but not by a sequence. This is often the only handicap to the serene progress of this game to a satisfactory conclusion.

Martha

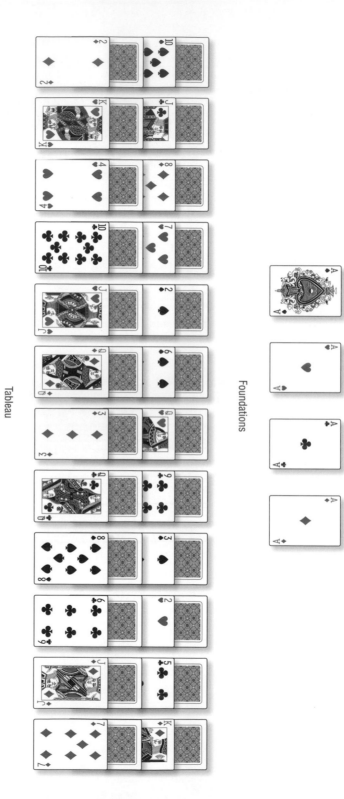

Tableau

Foundations

94

Example game

With the cards dealt as shown, the ♦2, 3 can be built immediately to the foundation, and the cards they were covering are turned over and exposed. The ♠2, ♠3, and ♥2, which can be seen in columns 5, 9 and 10, should be made available as soon as possible. To help free the two 2s, the ♣6 can be packed on ♦7 and ♥J on ♣Q, followed by the ♣10. This allows five cards from the third tier to be turned over, and the situation can be reviewed further. It would be unwise to pack the ♣Q and ♥J on to ♥K unless it becomes necessary, since one should try to get Kings to the top of columns, as they are blocking cards. It would be best to try to create a space by getting rid of a column, and then playing ♥K to it. If the Queen and Jack are played below the King, then it might require two columns to be cleared to get the King to the top because cards can be played to fill a space only singly.

Matrimony

It is often said that it takes hard work to make a successful marriage. The patience game Matrimony also takes lots of work, but is rarely as fruitful. It is recommended therefore only to those who can bear frustration and who prefer a game that it is a real challenge to get out.

Alternative names	None, but other patience games are also called Matrimony
Number of packs required	Two
Time needed to get it out	20 minutes
Prospects of success	About 1 in 30

Aim
To build eight foundations in suit sequence, three down to Queens, the fourth up to a Jack, and the other four down to Jacks.

Preparation
One ♦Q and one ♦J are removed from the pack and placed to the top of the space available as foundations. As they become available in play the two ♥Js are placed to the left of ♦J, and the four black 10s to the right of the ♦Q.

These cards will complete a foundation row of eight cards, in the order: ♥J, ♥J, ♦J, ♦Q, ♣10, ♣10, ♠10, ♠10.

Below the foundation row are dealt 16 cards in two rows of eight. This is the tableau (see illustration).

Play
The object is to build on the foundation cards in suit sequences, the three Jacks in descending order to Queens, the Queen in ascending order to Jack, and the four 10s in descending order to Jacks. The sequences are 'round the corner' ie Ace ranks above King and below 2.

All cards in the initial tableau are available and can be built to the foundation row, either as foundations themselves or built onto the existing foundations. Spaces in the tableau are not filled, but when all moves are made another 16 cards are dealt to the tableau, covering the first cards and the spaces. Further moves are made, with the top card in each pile being available, the playing of a card making the one below it available.

Play continues thus until all the stock is dealt, the last deal being of six cards only, which are dealt to the first six piles.

When play again comes to a standstill, the 16th pile is picked up and turned over to form a new stock, being dealt one card at a time beginning with the space it occupied and continuing to piles 1, 2, 3 etc. Further building is carried out as far as possible. The 15th pile is then taken up as the new stock and dealt as far as it will go too, beginning with the space it left, followed by piles 16, 1, 2, 3 etc.

Play continues in this manner until the first pile becomes the stock and is dealt out. If play again comes to a standstill before all the foundations are built up, the game is lost.

Example game

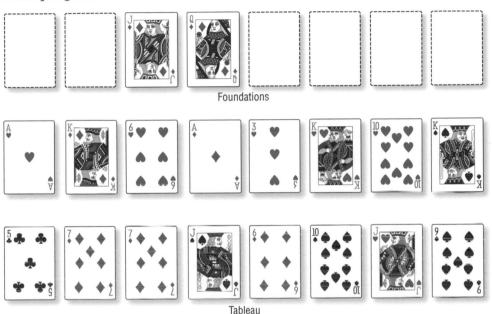

Foundations

Tableau

The initial deal is as illustrated, with the ♦J and ♦Q having been removed from the pack and allotted their places in the foundation row. The ♦K and ♦A can be built on the ♦Q foundation (this is the only foundation built in ascending order). The ♠10 is played to its foundation space and ♠9 built on it. The ♥J is played to its foundation space, followed by ♥10. These are the only moves possible, so the next 16 cards are dealt to the tableau and the game continues.

Miss Milligan

Miss Milligan has correctly been described as 'maddening'. But this refers to the game, not the person. The real Miss Milligan, although her name has graced this game for years, is elusive; no one knows who the original Miss Milligan was, if indeed she existed at all. Miss Milligan is a very difficult patience to get out, so is for those who enjoy a rare triumph, rather than those who like to succeed at least once each time they sit at the table to play.

Alternative names	None
Number of packs required	Two
Time needed to get it out	20 minutes
Prospects of success	About 1 in 20

Aim
To end with eight piles of cards, two for each suit, in sequence from Ace up to King.

Preparation
The two packs of cards are shuffled together, making a pack of 104 cards, and eight cards are dealt face up in a row. The remaining 96 cards are set aside, face down, for the time being.

Play
The eight cards dealt are all available for play. Aces are played to a foundation row above the initial eight cards as they become available, and the Aces should be built up with cards of the same suit, in sequence up to Kings, as they become available.

All available cards can also be packed on each other, one at a time, in downward sequences of alternate colours. A complete sequence can also be packed on another column in the same way.

When no further moves can be made, the pack is taken face down into the hand and another eight cards are dealt face up to the foot of the columns, from left to right, overlapping any cards which might be in the column. Again all possible moves are completed, and then another eight cards are dealt in the same way. Only the cards at the foot of each column are available for play. No packing or building can be done until all eight cards have been dealt to the row; in other words, it is not allowed to pack or build on a foundation, or place an Ace to a foundation, in the middle of dealing.

Should a column become vacant, it can only be filled by an exposed King, or an exposed sequence headed by a King.

There is one extra help for the player. When all the cards in the stock have run out (which they will do exactly after thirteen deals, there being thirteen eights in 104), the player may temporarily take into his hand any exposed card which is preventing him from making any moves. This is called 'waiving'. He can then make all the moves made possible by the removal of the card. However, once he has made these moves, he must be able to replace the waived card legally into the tableau, either by building to a foundation or packing. If he cannot, the game is lost.

If he can replace the card, then he may waive another card on the same conditions. He can waive as many cards as he likes, but only one at a time, and only if he can replace the waived card after making the moves available to him.

Example hand

Suppose the eight cards dealt are as illustrated.

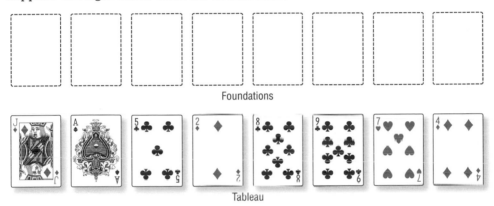

Foundations

Tableau

The ♠A is played to a foundation; ♥7 packed on ♣8; ♦4 packed on ♣5. That is all the moves that can be made at the moment. The tableau as it now stands is shown in the illustration that follows. You will notice that there are three blank columns. A blank column is always useful because an available King (but only a King), which later in the game might block a column, can be played to a blank column.

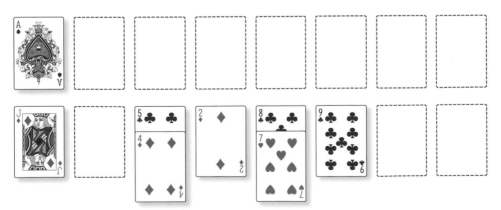

As no further moves can be made, another eight cards are dealt face up to the columns. Suppose these eight cards are ♦A, ♠6, ♥K, ♠10, ♠A, ♠Q, ♦8, ♦Q.

Now ♦A and ♠A (the second one) are played to foundations; ♠Q packed on ♥K, followed by ♦J and ♠10; ♦2 is built on its foundation; ♠6 is packed on ♥7; ♦8 is packed on ♣9. This ends the activity, but, as explained above, the sequence headed by ♥K can be moved to a blank column – let's say column 1. Another eight cards are now dealt from left to right. Suppose they are: ♥5, ♣8, ♥A, ♠9, ♣J, ♣K, ♦3, ♦10.

Now ♥A can be played to a foundation, ♦3 can be built on ♦2 in the foundation, followed by ♦4; ♦10 can be played to ♣J; thus allowing ♦Q to be packed on ♣K, followed by ♣J, ♦10 as a unit; now the whole sequence headed by ♣K can be played to a blank column; ♠9 can be packed on ♦10; ♥5 can be packed on ♠6.

The illustration above shows the tableau as it now stands. There are still two valuable blank columns. A further eight cards are now dealt, and so on. This game is going well – better than most.

Monte Carlo

Monte Carlo is a fairly mechanical patience game, but it can be addictive, as it keeps coming so close to being got out that the player is tempted into having another go.

Alternative names	Double and Quits, Wedding
Number of packs required	One
Time needed to get it out	Eight minutes
Prospects of success	About one in six

Aim
To eliminate all the cards in pairs from the table.

Preparation
The cards are shuffled and five rows of five cards are dealt left to right one below the other (see illustration overleaf). This forms the tableau.

Play
Any two adjacent cards of the same rank, positioned either side to side, top to bottom, or corner to corner, are picked up and discarded. The removal of a card does not make the cards each side of it adjacent.

When all such pairs have been removed, the remaining cards are consolidated, ie are all moved forward to fill the gaps, while being kept in the order in which they were originally dealt. That is, if there are gaps in the top row, the right-hand cards are moved to the left to fill them, with cards from the left hand side of the second row moved up to the right-hand side of the first row and so on (see Example game below).

When the tableau is consolidated, cards from the stock are dealt to it until the five rows of five are restored, and the operation is repeated. Play continues like this until the stock is exhausted (the last deal of the stock will probably be insufficient to complete the 5 x 5 pattern).

Cards continue to be discarded after the stock is exhausted, and each time play comes to a standstill the tableau is consolidated. The game is won if all cards are discarded.

Example game
The cards are dealt as in the illustration overleaf.

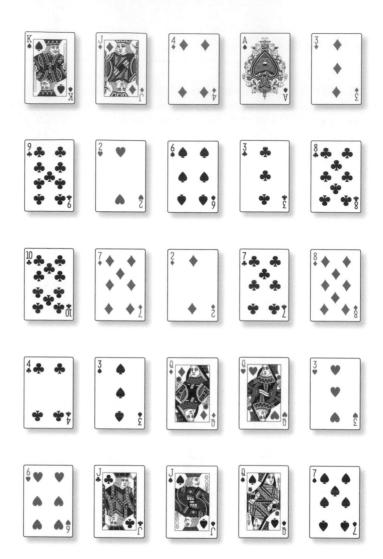

The ♦3 and ♣3 are discarded. The ♥2 and ♦2 are discarded (note that the removal of ♦2 does not make ♦7 and ♣7 adjacent). Also discarded are ♣8 and ♦8 and ♣J and ♠J. Any two of ♥Q, ♦Q and ♠Q can be discarded. The player should choose ♥Q and ♦Q, since when the tableau is consolidated, ♠3 and ♥3 will thus become adjacent.

When consolidating, the ♣9 moves to the right-hand side of the top row, the ♠6 moves to the extreme left of the second row, followed by ♣10, ♦7, ♣7 and ♣4, the third row becomes ♠3, ♥3, ♥6, ♠Q and ♠7. This leaves two rows empty at the foot and ten cards are dealt from the stock to fill. The two 3s have come together as predicted and the ♣7 can be removed with either ♦7 or ♠7… and so on.

Mount Olympus

Mount Olympus has been a very popular patience for more than 100 years. The tableau resembles the mountain where the Greek gods lived, while the foundation cards are the clouds surrounding it, and when the patience is got out, as it should be, the mountain has disappeared and the clouds have become 16 shining Greek gods and goddesses (the Kings and Queens) looking down to earth.

Alternative names	None
Number of packs required	Two
Time needed to get it out	20 minutes
Prospects of success	About two in three

Aim
To end with a semi-circle of piles of cards with alternate Kings and Queens at the top, each built up in a suit sequence of twos from an Ace or 2.

Preparation
All the Aces and 2s are removed from the two packs and arranged in a semi-circle of alternating Aces and 2s by suit (see illustration overleaf). These 16 cards are the foundations. A fairly large space is required, but see under Variant for a more compact layout. The remaining cards are shuffled and nine are dealt out in the form of a pyramid beneath the foundation cards. They are dealt from top to bottom and left to right. This is the tableau. There should be plenty of space left in the tableau as these cards will be packed upon.

Play
The foundations are to be built up with alternately sequenced cards, ie the Aces up to Kings in the sequence A, 3, 5, 7, 9, J, K, and the 2s up to Queens in the sequence 2, 4, 6, 8, 10, Q.

All the cards in the tableau are available for play to the foundations. They are also available to be packed onto each other in descending suit sequence by gaps of two, eg 9, 7, 5. A sequence can be packed as a whole unit from one tableau pile to another provided the join with the second pile maintains the suit sequence by gaps of two. The top card of each pile is always available.

When a space in the tableau is created by all the cards in the pile being moved, it is filled immediately by the top card of the stock (not by a card or cards already in the tableau).

When the initial layout is completed, and all possible building on the foundations or packing on tableau piles has been completed, with all spaces filled, another nine cards are dealt to each tableau pile, in the same top to bottom order as before, and further moves are made.

Mount Olympus

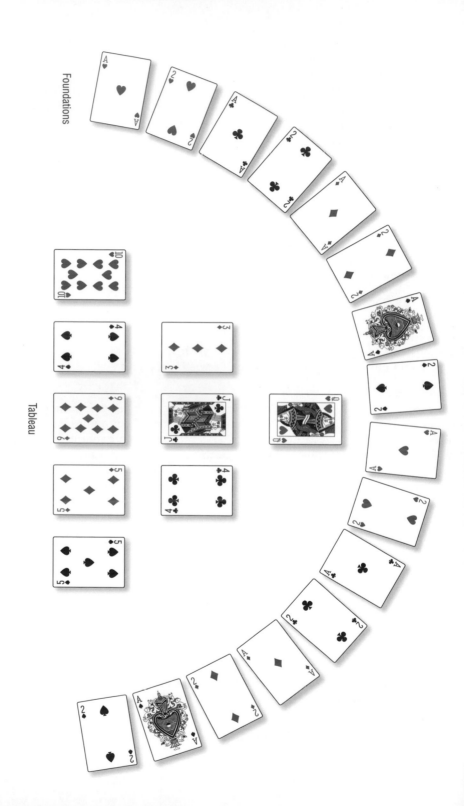

A fresh nine cards are dealt to the tableau whenever play comes to a standstill, until the stock is exhausted (in the last round there might not be enough cards to go round all the piles). There is no redeal. If all cards cannot be played to foundations, the game is lost.

Example game

The illustration shows a game about to begin after the deal. The ♦3 and ♦5 can be played to the ♦A foundation, and the ♣4 and ♠4 to the ♣2 and ♠2 foundations. The ♥10 can be packed on the ♥Q. The five spaces created are filled by the top five cards from the stock, which may allow other moves to be made. When the tableau is finally restored to nine piles and play comes to a standstill, nine further cards are dealt, one to each tableau pile, and play resumes.

Variant

If space is limited, the foundation cards can be arranged in two rows of eight, and the tableau in one row of nine beneath them. This makes for more manageable play – but the romance of the game is lost.

Odd and Even

Odd and Even is an unusual patience game, success in which is dependent on nothing more than luck, with few decisions left to the player. But concentration is necessary because the foundations build up in a strange manner.

Alternative names	None
Number of packs required	Two
Time needed to get it out	Twelve minutes
Prospects of success	About one in ten

Aim
To build up eight foundations by gaps of two, so that one row of four foundations is built from Aces to Queens, and the other from 2s to Kings.

Preparation
The two packs are shuffled, and three rows of three cards are dealt to form a reserve. Space is required above the reserve for two rows of four foundation cards.

Play
The foundations, as they become available, are one Ace and one 2 of each suit. All nine cards in the reserve are available to play to the foundations. A card played from the reserve to a foundation is immediately replaced by the top card of the waste heap, or the stock if there is no waste heap.

The remainder of the combined pack, the stock, is turned over one card at a time, and played to a foundation, if possible, or if not possible, is played to a single waste heap, the top card of which is always available for play.

It is convenient to have the Ace foundations on the top row, and the 2 foundations on the second row, with each 2 placed below the Ace of its suit (see illustration).

Each foundation is built up by gaps of two as follows:

Ace foundations: A, 3, 5, 7, 9, J, K, 2, 4, 6, 8, 10, Q

2 foundations: 2, 4, 6, 8, 10, Q, A, 3, 5, 7, 9, J, K

It will be noticed that at the beginning of the game, the top row is built with odd-numbered ranks, and the bottom row by even-numbered ranks, but that towards the end of the game this is reversed. This is where concentration is required of the player, especially as the piles build up at different rates, and it is not uncommon for identical cards to be heading both foundations of a suit. When this happens, the same card is required for both piles, and the player chooses on which pile to play it. One redeal is allowed. The waste heap is picked up and turned over without being shuffled, and is redealt. An annoying thing about this game is that while the odds of success are about ten to one, if a second redeal were to be allowed then the game would more often be got out. But rules are rules...

Example game

The illustration shows a game in the early stages. The ♦2 and ♣2 have been played to their foundations, as have ♣A and ♥A. The ♣2 has had ♣4 added, and the ♥A has been built up to ♥5. Next, the newly dealt top card of the waste heap, the ♦A should be played to its foundation, and the ♦3 built on it. The space thus created in the reserve is filled by the newly exposed top card of the waste heap.

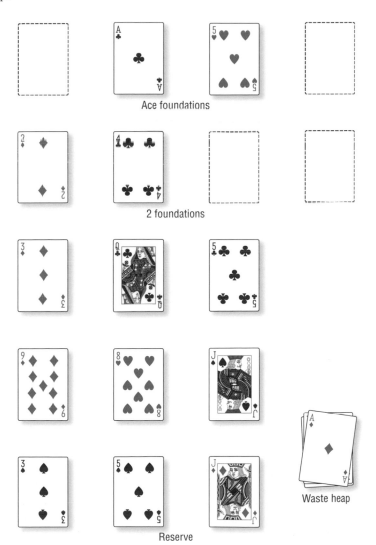

Ace foundations

2 foundations

Waste heap

Reserve

One Foundation

Its name perfectly describes this simple but addictive game – all the cards are built on one foundation. It deserves to be better known, since it is quite different from most other games of patience, and while it is not easy to get out, hope usually remains right to the end.

Alternative names	None
Number of packs required	One
Time needed to get it out	Six minutes
Prospects of success	About 1 in 20

Aim
To build all the cards in the tableau to a single foundation before the stock runs out; in effect, to end with the whole pack built on the foundation.

Preparation
The pack is thoroughly shuffled, especially between a series of games. Thirty-five cards are built in seven columns of five overlapping cards (see illustration). There is a traditional way of doing this, and card players ought to do things in the traditional way. This is that a row of seven is dealt left to right, the second row of seven overlapping cards is dealt right to left, the third (and fifth) rows are dealt left to right and the fourth right to left.

Play
The cards at the foot of the columns (ie those not overlapped) are available for play and, as a card is played, then the card below it becomes available.

When the tableau has been dealt, the top card of the 17-card stock is turned and laid sideways below the tableau. This card is the foundation.

Available cards can be built upon the foundation in either ascending or descending sequence, irrespective of suit or colour. The sequence can go up and down at will with the one restriction: that Aces cannot be built on Kings or vice versa. A 2 is the only card that can be built on an Ace, and a Queen the only card that can be built on a King.

When the initial foundation card is laid, and all possible cards from the tableau built upon it, the next card from the stock is played to the foundation, and the process is repeated. When a column from the tableau is cleared, the space is not filled.

The object is to build the whole pack onto the foundation, but as the stock can always be played to the foundation, the object can be seen as getting all the cards in the tableau built to the foundation, as any cards remaining in the hand as stock can be played to the foundation anyway. So the game becomes a race to clear the tableau before the stock runs out.

It is an interesting game in that there are often alternative plays available at the turn of a stock card, and the player must choose which to take. It is interesting, too, near the end, if, say, there are two or three cards left in the tableau and two or three cards in the stock, the player can work out what ranks he needs the stock cards to be, and if so inclined can work out his chances of getting them.

Example game

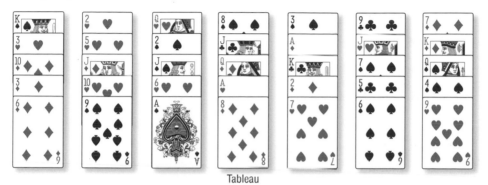

Tableau

Foundation

The tableau has been dealt as in the illustration, and the foundation card is the ♣8. There are two 9s and a 7 which could be played. One sequence could go ♥9, ♦8, ♥7, ♠6, ♣5, ♠4. Another sequence could be ♠9, ♥10, ♦J. Perhaps best would be ♠9, ♥10, ♥9, ♦8, ♥7, ♠6, ♣5, ♦6, ♠7, thus building nine cards to the foundation. The author followed this plan, and finished the game with seven cards still on the table.

Osmosis

Osmosis is an odd name for a patience game, and an odd game it is too, since the foundations are built on in no particular order of rank. This does not make it an easy game to get out, however, but it makes it an interesting one.

Alternative names	Treasure Trove
Number of packs required	One
Time needed to get it out	Ten minutes
Prospects of success	One in ten

Aim
To finish with four overlapping rows of 13 cards, one for each suit, in no particular order except that the left-hand foundation cards are of the same rank.

Preparation
The pack is shuffled and 16 cards are dealt face down into four piles of four. The piles are squared up, turned face up and placed in a column to the left (see illustration). These piles are reserves. The point of dealing them face down is that the player must not know which cards are in the piles. The next card is placed face up to the right of the top pile. This is the first foundation card.

Play
As the three cards of the same rank as the foundation card become available they are placed in a column below the first foundation. Cards at the top of the reserve piles are available for play, and as they are built to foundations, the cards below them become available. When the reserve piles are emptied they are not replaced. The stock is turned over in batches of three and played to a waste heap. The top card of the waste heap is always available for play. (The last batch might be of one or two cards only.) The object is to build onto each foundation card all the cards of the same suit. There is one vital condition – a card cannot be played to its foundation until the card of the same rank has been built to the foundation row above it. When the stock has all been played to the waste heap, the waste heap is turned over without shuffling and dealt again. There is no limit to the number of redeals, but when a whole redeal has been completed without a card being played to the foundations, the game is lost.

Example game
The game in progress, shown in the illustration, will explain the principle. The first foundation card was the ♦6, and a number of diamonds have been built to the foundation. The ♣6 was the second foundation card to become available, and the ♣7 and ♣A have been built on it, as the ♦7 and ♦A have already been

played to the diamond foundation. The ♥6 was the latest foundation card to appear. The ♦Q has just been dealt to the waste heap. This is built on the diamonds foundation. This allows the ♣Q to be built from the reserve to the clubs foundation, which could not be built to its foundation before the ♦Q was built. Similarly, the ♥8 cannot be played to its foundation from the reserve until the ♣8 is played to the club foundation. When the ♠6 is available it becomes the final foundation card, but the ♠7 in the reserve pile cannot be played to it before ♥7 is built to its respective foundation.

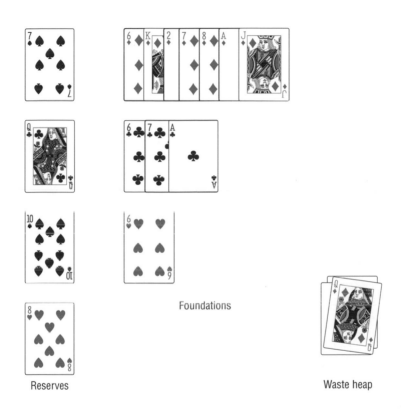

Foundations

Reserves

Waste heap

Pas Seul

Pas Seul is a ballet term meaning a dance for one, and so is a perfect name for a patience game. It is one of the simpler games in which cards are built up on the foundations to Kings but it is satisfying nonetheless because it often comes with a run at the end as a formidable waste heap rapidly disappears.

Alternative names	None
Number of packs required	One
Time needed to get it out	Eight minutes
Prospects of success	About one in five

Aim
To finish with the four suits in separate piles all built up from Ace to King.

Preparation
The pack is shuffled and a row of six cards is dealt to the table to form the tableau.

Play
If any cards in the tableau are Aces, they are immediately placed above the tableau to begin a foundation row of Aces. The spaces are filled from the top card of the stock to maintain the number of piles in the tableau at six.

Thereafter, Aces are played to the foundation row as they appear, and the object is to build the Aces up to Kings in suit sequence as cards become available. As well as being played to foundations, cards in the tableau can be packed on each other in descending sequence of alternate red and black cards. Again, spaces are filled from the top card of the stock. Sequences can be played from one pile to another provided the correct sequence is maintained.

When all possible moves have been made after the initial deal, the stock is turned over one card at a time and if possible each card is played to a foundation or to the tableau. If this is impossible, the card is played to a waste heap, the top card of which is always available for play, and can be used to fill a space in preference to the top card of the stock (but the top card cannot be looked at before the decision is made).

The game is lost if the stock is exhausted and the game is at a standstill. A redeal of the waste heap is not allowed.

Perpetual Motion

This is a well-named patience game that players either love or hate. It is very repetitive, and the tableau, if it can be called such, consists of four piles only, to which the player deals four cards over and over for anything up to an hour. A comfortable chair is recommended.

Alternative names	Narcotic
Number of packs required	One
Time needed to get it out	Up to an hour
Prospects of success	About one in four

Aim
To discard all the cards onto a waste pile.

Preparation
The pack is thoroughly shuffled and taken face down into the hand. A row of four cards is dealt face up.

Play
If two or more cards in the initial row are of the same rank, the leftmost of the equal cards remains where it is and the other(s) are moved to cover it. Then another row of four cards are dealt to the piles, filling any spaces that might have arisen. Once again if any cards are duplicated in rank they are piled upon the furthermost left of the equal cards. Four more cards are then dealt to the piles, and when all possible moves have been made, another four, and so on until the pack is exhausted (the last card dealt will always be on the fourth pile – if it isn't there has been a misdeal somewhere).

Cards can be moved only when a row of four has been dealt; in other words, cards cannot be moved while the deal is in progress. But after the deal, the moving of a card might expose another card that can be moved, and this is legal. Thus, for example, two cards of equal rank on top of the third pile can be moved together to a card of the same rank on top of the first pile, say, which might expose a card on the third pile which could be moved to the second.

If, on one deal, four cards of the same rank appear on top of each of the four piles, the four cards are removed to a waste pile and take no further part.

When all the cards in the hand have been dealt, the pile to the right is picked up and placed face up on its neighbour to the left, the combined pile is then moved face up to the pile to its left, and the new combined pile moved face up to the first pile.

This pile is then turned over and taken in hand, and the whole process repeated. There is no limit to the number of redeals. Very gradually, cards of the same rank tend to come together, and eventually four of the same rank will appear on top of the piles and be discarded. It might take several minutes to discard the first batch of four, but with luck the discarding will speed up. The game is won if all the cards can be discarded in 13 batches of four of the same rank.

Sometimes, once the pack has been reduced to eight cards, it becomes clear that the cards are in such an order that the game will never come out – the pattern of the four piles will repeat itself from time to time in an endless loop. That is the time to give in (or you might decide to give in after an hour's play!).

Warning: It is essential to take care in making sure all possible moves are made, and that the cards are picked up correctly after each deal. It is annoying if a disarrangement of the cards or a misdeal ruins half-an-hour's effort.

Pyramid

Pyramid is a game with a very pleasing tableau, which ensures its presence in most collections of patience games. But beware – it can be infuriating. The chances of getting it out are only about 1 in 50. The game takes only five minutes or so, but one can play for the same number of hours without reward if unlucky.

Alternative names	Pile of Twenty-eight
Number of packs required	One
Time needed to get it out	Six minutes
Prospects of success	About 1 in 50

Aim
To finish with all the cards in a discard pile.

Preparation
The cards are dealt face up in the form of a pyramid of seven rows, increasing from one card at the apex to seven at the base, with each card except those on the bottom row being overlapped by two other cards. The pyramid forms the tableau.

Play
The cards on the bottom row are available for play. As play proceeds, the removal of two adjacent cards in a row uncovers a card in the row above which becomes available for play.

From the initial tableau, pairs of available cards whose pip total equals 13, irrespective of suit, are removed. For this purpose Aces equal one, Jacks equal eleven and Queens equal twelve; Kings equal 13 and so are removed singly. Cards removed are placed to one side in a discard pile.

The remaining cards form the stock. When all possible cards have been paired and removed from the initial tableau, the stock is turned over one card at a time. If the card turned can be paired with an available card from the tableau, it is paired and discarded; if it is a King, it is discarded immediately on its own. If it cannot be paired, it is played face up to a 'talon'. The top card of the talon is always available and may be paired with the next card turned from the stock or with any available card in the pyramid.

The game is won if all the cards end in the discard pile, or lost if no further moves can be made. Once the stock is turned over, there is no redeal.

Example game

From the tableau illustrated, ♦K is removed to the discard pile. Other cards to be paired and played to the discard pile are ♦Q and ♦A, which releases ♣K to the discard pile. The ♠3 and ♠10 are also discarded, thus releasing ♦5 which can in turn be paired with ♥8 and discarded.

No more moves in the initial tableau can now be made and so the first card is turned from the stock. Suppose it is ♥9. This is paired with ♦4 and discarded, releasing ♣6 and ♦7 to be paired and discarded. Again no more moves can be made in the tableau and the next card is now turned from the stock. It is ♠8. This pairs with nothing, so begins the talon. The next card is turned from the stock… and so on.

Queen of Italy

Following our usual practice of naming patience games after high-born ladies when the opportunity arises, we will use Queen of Italy for this one, although it is probably better known as Terrace. It frequently rewards skill, with the added attraction that an accomplished player will succeed in getting it out more often than not.

Alternative names	Signora, Terrace
Number of packs required	Two
Time needed to get it out	20 minutes
Prospects of success	Experts, one in two; beginners, one in six

Aim
To finish with eight piles of 13 cards, all built up in ascending order of alternate colours. The rank of the foundations is decided by the player after the deal, and the sequences are 'round-the-corner', ie Ace follows King and precedes 2.

Preparation
After shuffling the two packs together eleven cards are dealt face up in a row, at the top of the available space, each overlapping the previous card. This is the terrace, which gives the game its alternative name. Below the terrace is dealt a row of four cards face up. From these one is chosen as the rank of the foundation cards. If two or more of the cards are of the same rank, then that rank might well be chosen as the foundation card, and if all four are of the same rank, then there is no option, they must be chosen as the foundations.

Usually, the four cards are of different rank, and one will be chosen by the player after studying the terrace (see under Strategy below). The chosen foundation card(s) is moved to a row below the terrace, and as other cards of that rank become available during play, they are moved to this row, which ultimately will contain eight piles with the foundation cards at the bottom. Of course, the card at the top of a completed foundation pile will be one rank lower than the card at the bottom. The rejected cards from the four from which the foundation rank was chosen are now placed below the foundation row and sufficient cards dealt to them to bring the row to nine.

The illustration on p119 shows a game at this stage. The ♣Q, ♣6, ♦A and ♣J are the four cards from which ♣6 was chosen as the foundation rank. The other three cards, with six others, form the tableau.

Play
The right-hand card in the terrace, ie the topmost card, is available for building to a foundation, but only to a foundation. It cannot be played to the tableau. When it is played, the card below it becomes available on the same terms. The cards

in the terrace are not replaced. Tableau cards may be played to foundations, in ascending order of rank in alternate colours. They may also be stacked on other tableau cards in descending order of rank and in alternate colours. Again the packing is 'round-the-corner' but this time King follows Ace. But they can only be moved one at a time, ie a sequence cannot be moved as a whole. Cards are packed overlapping each other so that the player can see all the cards in the column. Cards cannot be played back from the foundations to the tableau.

A space formed in the tableau by all the cards of a column being played, must be filled immediately, either from the top of a waste heap or by turning the top card of the stock (the two cards cannot be compared before a choice is made). Cards from the terrace or cards already in the tableau cannot be used to fill a space.

When all moves arising from the initial deal have been made, the stock is turned one card at a time to a single waste heap. The top card of the waste heap is always available for play. There is no redeal. The game is won when all foundation piles are built up in sequence.

Strategy An important decision comes at the beginning, when the foundation card must be chosen. This depends upon the terrace. You should not normally choose a rank that occurs more than once in the terrace or which occurs in the terrace towards the left, and therefore will not be available until the game is well advanced.

To be successful it is necessary to get rid of the terrace, so that should be a tactical priority, and packing in the tableau should have the aim of releasing the next card or two from the terrace.

Example game

The illustration shows the position after the choice of the foundation rank. The ♣6 was chosen as the first foundation, and the other three cards dealt to the tableau, ♣Q, ♦A and ♣J have had six other cards added to them.

The ♣6 was chosen as the foundation card since the available card at the end of the terrace, ♦6, can immediately be played to the foundation row, with the next terrace card, ♣7, built upon it. The main consideration now is to build up the ♦6 foundation to a black Jack, which will allow the ♥Q to be played from the terrace to the foundation and thus release a further foundation card, ♠6.

So the ♦6 and ♣7 are played to the foundation row. It is possible now to pack cards in the tableau. The maximum packing would be ♥10 on ♣J; ♠9 on ♥10; ♥J on ♣Q; ♣4 on ♥5, thus reducing the piles in the tableau to five and opening four spaces for new tableau cards. However, with the exception perhaps of packing ♣4 on ♥5 (since these cards will not be wanted for the foundations for some time) it might be better to start turning the stock and only packing in the tableau when a soon-wanted card appears. For example, if the first card turned were a 5, which will not be needed till near the end of the game, it could remain in the waste heap. If, on the other hand, it were a 7, 8, or 9, space could be made for it in the tableau by packing ♥10 on ♣J. Note that one should not pack the ♠9 on the ♥10 because, if another space were wanted, the pair of ♥10, ♠9 could not then be packed on ♣J, as cards can only be packed singly. For this reason, packing in the tableau should not be done earlier than necessary. The existing position is promising because, if a red 8 appears, it can be played to ♣7 in the foundation, and ♠9, ♥10 and ♣J could then follow, releasing the ♥Q from the terrace to the foundation and also the ♠6.

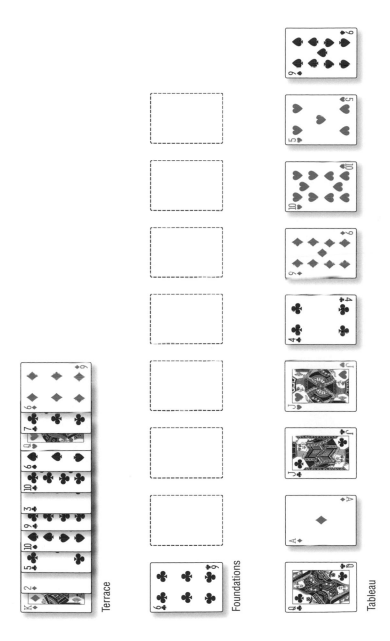

Terrace

Foundations

Tableau

Queen's Audience

This is a game for Royalists, since the object is to get all the cards from the ante-chamber into the audience chamber to meet their respective Queens. The variant (see below) called King's Audience is played when the monarch is male. It is a quick and simple game with an unusual and pleasing layout.

Alternative names	King's Audience (see below)
Number of packs required	One
Time needed to get it out	Five minutes
Prospects of success	About one in two

Aim

To finish with the four Queens, supported by their Kings, in a row above a pile of cards in their respective suits, built from Jack down to 2, with the Aces supporting them.

Preparation

The cards are shuffled, and 16 are dealt out in a square (see illustration). These are the walls of the audience chamber. Inside the audience chamber are two foundation rows, the upper row reserved for their respective Majesties, with the King supporting (ie underneath) the Queen, and the lower for their subjects, ie the rest of the suit with the Ace supporting the Jack through to 2.

Play

The cards in the walls of the audience chamber are available for play to the foundations. The upper row will contain the King and Queen of each suit, with the Queen uppermost. However, it is necessary that both the King and Queen are available for play simultaneously before they can be played to the foundation. Similarly, the lower foundations can only be begun when the Ace and Jack of a suit are simultaneously available, in which case they are played to the foundation, Jack uppermost.

When cards in the initial layout are played to their foundations, if any are available, they are replaced by cards from the stock.

The stock is then dealt one at a time to a waste heap. The top card of the waste heap as well as all the cards forming the walls of the audience chamber are available for play. When a card is played from the walls, it is replaced first by the top card of the waste heap, or if there is no waste heap, by the top card from the stock.

The game is won if all cards are played to foundations, in which case the walls of the audience chamber will have disappeared, and it is lost if all cards have been played to the waste heap and no other moves are possible. There is no redeal.

Example game

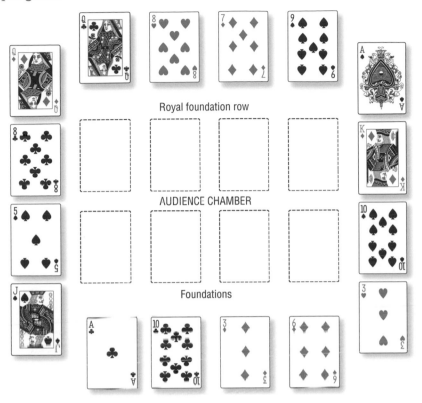

Royal foundation row

AUDIENCE CHAMBER

Foundations

The 16 cards forming the audience chamber are dealt as in the illustration. The
♦K can be played to the royal foundation row with the ♦Q on top. The ♠A can
be played with the ♠J above it to the lower foundation row. Immediately, the
♠10 and ♠9 can follow to the foundation. This removes six cards from the walls
of the audience chamber, and they are replaced by six cards from the top of the
stock, since there is not yet a waste heap. Any further moves made possible by
rebuilding the walls are then made. Notice that the ♣Q cannot be moved to a
foundation until the ♣K becomes available, and similarly the ♣A must remain
where it is until the ♣J becomes available.

When the wall is complete, and no further moves are possible, the first card is
turned to the waste heap, and is available. If it cannot be played, the next card
is turned and so on.

This game has begun promisingly. Usually if four or five cards in the initial layout
are Aces or court cards, and especially if two or more match, there is a good
chance of getting the game out.

Variant
King's Audience is played in exactly the same way, except that the Kings are
placed on top of the Queens in the upper foundation row.

Red and Black

Red and Black is for those who like a two-pack patience game in which there is plenty of action but relatively little thinking to be done, and the result will almost certainly be positive. This is perhaps why it is well known and popular.

Alternative names	Rouge et Noir
Number of packs required	Two
Time needed to get it out	Twelve minutes
Prospects of success	About five in six

Aim

To finish with eight piles, each built from Ace foundations up to Kings in ascending sequence of alternate colours.

Preparation

The eight Aces are removed from the packs and arranged in a row face up to form foundations. The two packs are well shuffled together to make one combined pack. A row of eight cards is dealt below the eight foundations, to form the tableau (see illustration).

Play

The foundations are to be built on in alternate colours up to Kings. Cards available are the top cards of the tableau piles. As well as being built to foundations, these cards may be packed on in descending order of alternate colours. They may be transferred from one pile to another, but only one card at a time, not in sequences. It is best, however, to pack them overlapping in columns, so that one can see how the game is developing.

The stock is taken in hand face down and dealt one card at a time face up to the table. Each card may be built to a foundation or to the tableau, and if this is impossible it is played to a single waste heap. The top card of the waste heap is always available for play.

If a space occurs in the tableau, it is filled immediately by the top card of the waste heap, or if there is not a waste heap, by the top card from the stock.

One redeal is permitted (it is not always necessary) by picking up the waste pile, turning it over and dealing again. It must not be shuffled.

Example game

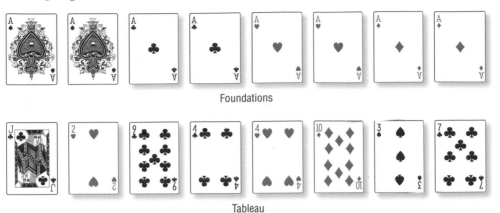

Foundations

Tableau

The Aces are set out in a row and the eight cards forming the tableau are dealt as shown. The ♥2 can be built to the ♠A (any black Ace would do), and the ♠3 and ♥4 follow to the same foundation. The ♦10 is packed on the ♣J and the ♣9 follows. Note that if the ♣9 had been packed on ♦10 first, then the two cards could not be packed on ♣J, since cards can be packed from one tableau pile to another only singly. This makes five spaces in the tableau which are filled from the top of the stock, there being as yet no waste heap. This may facilitate further moves. When all possible moves are made, the top card of the stock is played to the table and the game proceeds as described.

Variants

Methods have been suggested to make the game less easy, as follows:

i) A redeal is not allowed. To compensate, cards may be moved from pile to pile in the tableau in blocks, ie a sequence can be moved as a whole to another pile, provided the correct sequence between the two columns is maintained. This makes the game slightly more difficult to get out.

ii) The foundations may be built on only in ascending suit sequence, ie not in sequence of alternate colours. This makes the game much more difficult to get out, but by no means impossible, and it provides some exciting games as success often comes from seemingly hopeless positions.

Rosamund's Bower

'Fair Rosamund' Clifford was the mistress of Henry II. She lived in a royal palace at Woodstock in Oxfordshire, allegedly hidden away in a secret bower within a maze, to prevent her discovery by Eleanor of Aquitaine, who was Henry's wife.

The object of this game is to reunite Rosamund and Henry, and it is to be hoped that they themselves did not find it as frustrating a task as the players commemorating them might.

Alternative names	None
Number of packs required	One
Time needed to get it out	Ten minutes
Prospects of success	One in four

Aim

To finish with the whole pack in one pile with the ♠J at the bottom and the cards in descending sequence, irrespective of suit, with King following Ace, to ♣K and ♥Q at the top.

Preparation

The ♥Q, ♣K and ♠J are removed from the pack. The ♥Q is placed in the centre of the table.

The pack is shuffled and eight cards are dealt, two to each side of the ♥Q, as in the illustration. The ♣K is placed to the upper right of the tableau, and the ♠J to the lower right. Seven cards are dealt face down in a pile to the right of the ♣K.

The ♥Q represents Rosamund in her bower, with the surrounding cards her guards. The ♣K is Henry II, and the seven face-down cards beside him are reserve guards. The object is to reunite Rosamund and the King atop the whole pack above the ♠J, which is the foundation.

Play

Cards are built on to the foundation in descending order of rank, irrespective of suit, in one long continuous sequence, King following Ace.

The stock is taken in hand face down, and cards are turned one at a time and either built onto the foundation or to one of three waste heaps, according to choice. The top card of each waste heap is always available to play to the foundation, but cards cannot be transferred from one waste heap to another.

Also available are the cards on the outside of the eight cards protecting the Queen, and these must be played to the foundation immediately, ie in preference to a card on top of a waste heap. When one of the cards surrounding the Queen is played, it is immediately replaced by the top card from the reserve pile next to the ♣K. Note that if the inner card surrounding the Queen is of one rank lower than the outer card, and could thus follow it to the foundation, it cannot do so, as the outer card must be replaced from the reserve immediately. Only when the outer card is played and the reserve is exhausted does the inner card become the outer card and therefore available. When the reserve is exhausted, the cards surrounding the Queen are not replaced when used, and eventually, if the game is to be got out, all these cards will disappear to the foundation.

When the stock in hand is exhausted, the waste heaps may be picked up in any order to form a new stock, but must not be shuffled. The stock is taken in hand face down and dealt to the foundation or waste heaps as before.

The waste heaps may be collected and redealt in the same way twice more. The game is won if the foundation is built up to the final Ace, which is followed by ♣K and ♥Q.

Strategy The governing of the waste heaps is the crucial matter. The player should try to build upward sequences in each waste heap, so that they can be played to the foundation in reverse order when the opportunity occurs. However, the cards on the outside of those guarding the Queen should be borne in mind, as it is pointless to build up a sequence to, say, an 8 if there is an 8 available in the tableau, since the 8 from the tableau must be played first to the foundation, and the sequence cannot then follow it.

Example game
The tableau is dealt as in the illustration overleaf.

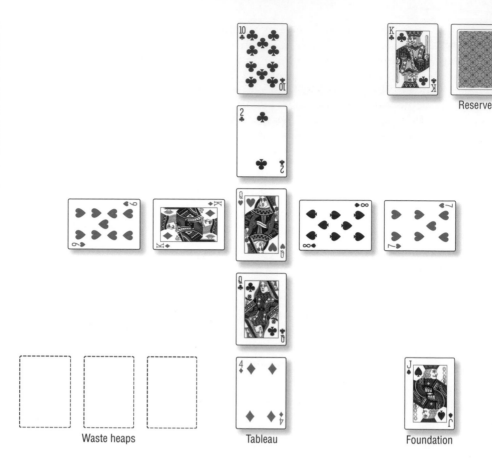

Waste heaps   Tableau   Foundation

Before the stock is turned from hand, ♣10 is played to the foundation, and replaced with the top card of the reserve. The ♥9 is played to the foundation, and replaced from the reserve. Unless one of the two cards from the reserve was an 8, the cards must now be turned from the stock in hand. Note that the ♠8 cannot yet be played to the foundation as it is not an outside card of those guarding ♥Q. Cards must now be played from stock to the three waste heaps until an 8 appears, when it is played to the foundation, followed by ♥7, which is replaced from the reserve, and so on.

Royal Rendezvous

Royal Rendezvous is a well-known game in which twelve foundations are built up in different ways – some singly and some in twos. It requires concentration rather than skill, and has the pleasing property that it can be got out from what, even near the end, seem to be impossible situations.

Alternative names	None
Number of packs required	Two
Time needed to get it out	20 minutes
Prospects of success	About one in two

Aim
To build up twelve foundations, four in single suit sequence from Ace to Queen, four in twos from Ace to King, and a final four in twos from 2 to Queen, and position four spare Kings so that at the end there is a grand royal rendezvous at the top of their piles of eight Kings and eight Queens.

Preparation
The eight Aces and four 2s, one of each suit, are removed from the pack. One Ace from each suit is arranged in a row, with the other Ace of its suit below it. On each side of the bottom row are arranged the 2s, for convenience in the same suit order as the Aces (see illustration).

The remaining cards are shuffled, and below the foundations are dealt face up 16 cards in two rows of eight, as in the illustration. These form the tableau.

Play
All four Aces on the top foundation row are to be built up in single suit sequence from Ace to Queen. The Aces in the second row are to be built up in suit sequence of two, from Ace to King, ie A, 3, 5, 7, 9, J, K. The 2s in the foundation are to be built in suit sequence of two, from 2 to Queen, ie 2, 4, 6, 8, 10, Q. This leaves four Kings unaccounted for, and these are to be played, as they become available, two to each end of the top foundation row, with the proviso that a King cannot be played there until its duplicate has been already played to a foundation in the second row.

All cards in the tableau are available at all times for building on their foundations. A card played from tableau to foundation is replaced by the top card of the waste heap or, if no waste heap exists, the top card of the stock.

When all moves possible have been made after the initial deal, and any spaces in the tableau refilled, the stock is turned over one card at a time, and any card which cannot be played to a foundation is played to a single waste heap, the top card of which is always available for play.

Example game

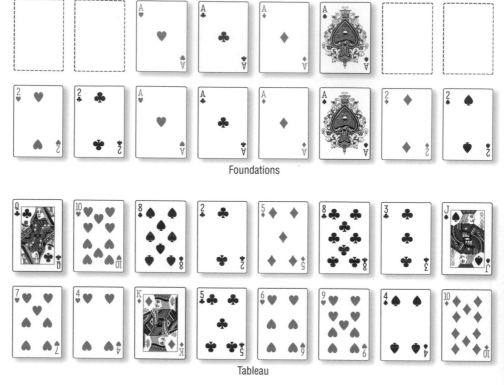

Foundations

Tableau

The illustration shows the initial layout immediately after the deal. The four blank spaces are for the four Kings, one of each suit, which will not be built to a foundation. Notice that at the initial deal, any 2, 3 or 4 can be played to a foundation. In the illustration, the ♥4 and ♥6 can be played to the ♥2 foundation, the ♠4 can be played to the ♠2 foundation, and the ♣2 can be played to its Ace foundation. This allows a choice of foundation for ♣3, which can either follow ♣2 onto the Ace foundation in the top row, or be played to the ♣A foundation in the bottom row. It might be best to choose the latter option, as ♣5 could then be played to it. The spaces in the tableau are filled and when any other possible moves are made, the top card is dealt from stock.

Variant

Some players prefer to build the Aces in the top row up to Kings rather than stopping at Queens. This means that the four spare Kings are incorporated into the building, and the game ends with twelve piles, eight built to Kings and four to Queens. It makes the game slightly more difficult to get out, and the game as described is preferred.

St Helena

Although Napoleon played cards while in exile on St Helena, the idea that he played numerous patience games seems to have been based on a misunderstanding. This has not prevented a whole range of patience games being invented which carry either his name or the name of the island. This particular one is an easy two-pack patience which should nearly always be got out.

Alternative names	Napoleon's Favourite, Washington's Favourite
Number of packs required	Two
Time needed to get it out	20 minutes
Prospects of success	About seven in eight

Aim
To finish with the four Kings built on in descending suit sequence to the Aces, and the four Aces built on in ascending suit sequence to the Kings.

Preparation
The four Kings and the four Aces are removed from one pack and arranged in two rows as foundations. The remaining cards are added to the other pack and the new combined pack of 96 cards is shuffled. The cards are dealt one at a time, face up, around the rows clockwise in twelve piles, beginning with the top left corner. There will be eight cards in each pile. These form the tableau.

Play
The top cards of the piles in the tableau are available for play to the foundations, with these restrictions: the cards in piles 1 to 4 (at the top of the tableau) may be built only on to the Kings, and the cards in piles 7 to 10 (at the foot of the tableau) only to the Aces. The cards in the piles at the side of the tableau – piles 5, 6, 11 and 12 – may be played to any foundation.

In addition, available cards can be packed from one tableau pile to another in descending or ascending sequence irrespective of suit or colour. The sequence may go up or down at will, ie the direction can be reversed in the same pile; for example, 3, 4, 5, 4, 3 and so on. However, the sequence is not 'round-the-corner'; only a 2 can be packed on an Ace, and only a Queen on a King. Only one card at a time may be moved, not sequences (ie only the top card is available). A space caused by the whole pile being played is not refilled (except by a redeal, as described below).

Redeals All possible moves are made. When no further play is possible, the cards in the tableau are collected up in reverse order to that in which they were dealt; for example, pile 12 is picked up first (face up), pile 11 added on top of it, and so on. When all the piles are picked up and the combined pile is turned face down, the top cards will be those that were originally in pile 12. The cards are now redealt without shuffling, face up, one at a time clockwise to the twelve spaces as at the beginning of play. Play continues as before, except that restrictions which prevent cards from certain tableau piles being built on certain foundations are lifted, and the top card of any pile is available to be played to any foundation.

A second redeal is allowed, but if all cards are not on the foundations at the end of that redeal the game is lost.

Example game

With the cards as dealt in the illustration, ♥2 can be built on ♥A, but ♦2 cannot be built on ♦A. Similarly, ♣Q can be built on ♣K but ♦Q cannot be built on ♦K. However, ♦Q can be packed on ♥J in pile 4, and thus becomes eligible for building on ♦K. It will be noticed that once ♥2 is built to its foundation, ♥3 can follow, but it would be better to pack ♦2 on ♥3 because from there it can be built on ♦A, after which ♥3 and ♥4 can be built to the foundation. The moving of these cards will expose others which become available for play.

Salic Law

This double-pack patience game requires the eight Queens to be discarded and take no part in the action at all. This is why it is called Salic Law, after the code which excluded women from succession to the throne in certain European countries like Spain and France. However, in these more enlightened times some players like to place the eight Queens in a row across the top of the tableau so that if the game succeeds they end by looking down in haughty fashion at a row of Jacks and a row of Kings.

Alternative names	None
Number of packs required	Two
Time needed to get it out	20 minutes
Prospects of success	About one in three

Aim
To end with eight piles of cards, irrespective of colour or suit, each in sequence from Ace up to Jack.

Preparation
The two packs of cards are shuffled together and the eight Queens removed, leaving a pack of 96 cards. The eight Queens are then placed in a row across the top of the tableau.

Play
One King (of any suit) is taken from the pack and placed below the left-hand Queen, with enough space between them to place another card; between the two will eventually be placed an Ace, which will begin a foundation row. Enough space should be left below the King for a column of overlapping cards of up to 20 or so to be built below it.

The cards are shuffled, and onto the first King is dealt a column of overlapping cards, face up, until another King appears, which is placed beside the first one to head a new column. The Aces, as soon as they appear, are played immediately to a foundation row between the Kings and the row of Queens.

Once an Ace has been built to the foundation row, a 2 of any suit can be built on it as soon as one appears in the deal, followed by a 3 when one appears, and so on, so the building is actually in progress while the deal continues.

When the cards being added to the second King to form a column arrive at a third King, then a third column is begun, and so on.

When the deal is complete, there will be a row of eight Queens at the top of the tableau, a row of eight Aces below, many of them already built on to varying levels, and a row of eight Kings below that, most or all of them with columns of overlapping cards descending from them.

The play then continues with the top cards (ie those at the foot of the columns) available for play to the foundations. When a bare King appears (ie all the cards in its column have been played to foundations) the column is deemed to be vacant, and any available card may be moved there to fill the vacancy (this privilege is open only when the deal is complete, and vacancies are not filled while the deal is in progress).

Vacancies can prove vital as the game progresses, and it is an advantage if at least one can be created during the dealing. This can be done by trying to vary the speed at which the foundations are built during the deal. A good tip is not to build the foundations too high during the deal – not beyond five, say.

Example game

The illustration shows the situation of a game immediately after the deal. The ♥6 and ♣6 can be built on the first two foundations, the ♣5 can be built on ♥4, releasing ♥4 to be built on ♥3. The ♣3 can be built to ♦2 and so on. It will be possible to make vacancies on the last two Kings, giving a prospect of getting the game out.

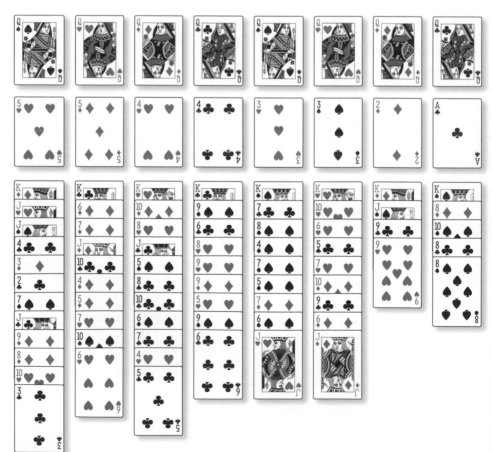

Sir Tommy

One of Sir Tommy's alternative names is Old Patience, and this game has certainly been around for a long time. It is the simplest of games, and requires no elaborate preparations: one just picks up the cards and starts.

Alternative names	Old Patience, Try Again
Number of packs required	One
Time needed to get it out	Five minutes
Prospects of success	About one in eight

Aim
To end with four piles of cards in ascending sequence from Ace to King, irrespective of suit or colour.

Preparation
The cards are shuffled and taken face down into the hand.

Play
Cards are turned over one at a time and played face up to four waste piles until an Ace appears, when it is played to a foundation row above the waste piles. The cards can be played to whichever waste pile the player chooses, and the card at the top of each waste pile is available for play. Once an Ace is played to a foundation, any available 2, of any colour or suit, can be played to it, and then any available 3 and so on up to King. Each Ace, as it appears, is played to a foundation and built upon.

Once played to a waste pile a card cannot be moved until it is built on a foundation. The cards in the waste piles can be overlapping, so that the player can see what cards each pile contains. There is no packing from one waste pile to another.

The game is won when all four foundations are built up to Kings. It is unsuccessful if all the cards have been played to the four waste piles and none of the cards available at the top of the waste piles can be built to foundations.

Strategy It is a good idea, if possible, to keep one waste pile for high-ranking cards like Kings. It is best if cards played to a waste pile can be placed on a higher-ranking card rather than a lower-ranking card, but this, of course, is not always possible. Cards of the same rank should be kept in different waste piles, if possible.

To succeed, this patience needs the Aces to appear fairly early on. It can be very infuriating when waste piles get large and unmanageable while the Aces refuse to appear. However, if the game fails it takes only seconds to collect the cards, shuffle them, and, as one of its alternative names suggests, Try Again.

Example game

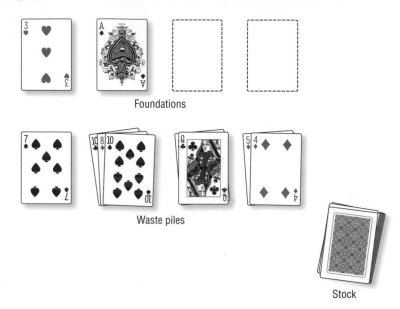

Foundations

Waste piles

Stock

The illustration shows a game in progress. Two Aces have been played to the foundation row, and the first has been built up to a 3. In fact, the 3 was the last card to be turned from the stock, and the 4 and 5 from the fourth waste pile can now be played to the same foundation.

Spider

Spider is a patience game which, according to *Redbook Magazine*, was the favourite of Franklin D Roosevelt, the four-times president of the USA, and the president during World War II. It is a game which is played in different ways, but the following description is that most commonly found in US books of the time, and likely to be the version played by Roosevelt.

Alternative names	None
Number of packs required	Two
Time needed to get it out	20 minutes
Prospects of success	About one in four

Aim
To end with eight piles of cards, in descending suit sequence from King down to Ace.

Preparation
The two packs of cards are shuffled together making a pack of 104 cards. The cards rank from King (high) to Ace (low).

A row of ten face-down cards is dealt to the table from the pack. Three further face-down rows are dealt to them, each card overlapping the card below, making ten columns. Then another face-down card is dealt to each of the first four columns. Finally, a face-up card is dealt to each column. The tableau therefore contains 54 cards, as illustrated on p137. The remaining 50 are placed to one side, face down, as the stock.

Play
The ten piles serve as both tableau and foundations. The top card of each column (ie the face-up card at its foot) is always available for play. Available cards may be built upon in descending order, regardless of suit, from King to Ace. An Ace cannot be built upon at all.

Cards can be played from one column to another singly, unless there is a sequence of the same suit in correct descending order at the foot of a column, when it can be moved as a whole to any card at the foot of another column, provided the correct descending sequence is maintained, ie ♥7, 6, 5 can be built upon any 8.

A face-down card at the foot of a column, exposed because the face-up cards which overlapped it have been moved elsewhere, is turned face up and becomes available for play.

A space created by the removal of a whole column may be filled by any available card or suit sequence from another column. Since a King cannot be played to an Ace, it may be moved only to a space created when all the cards in a column have been played elsewhere.

The object is to build a whole suit of 13 cards, in correct sequence from King down to Ace, within the tableau. When this is achieved the pile is removed, and discarded to one side. It is not obligatory to do this immediately – it may be used to help in further operations in the tableau. The game is won if all the cards can be removed from the tableau in eight separate piles of suit sequences from King down to Ace.

When all the moves have been made in the initial tableau (and any spaces which might be created are filled), the stock is taken in hand and ten cards are dealt face up to the foot of each column, overlapping the card previously at the foot. These cards immediately become available, and the remainder of the stock is set aside while further building takes place in the tableau. While dealing a row of ten cards to an existing tableau, no moves are allowed. The whole row has to be dealt before any manipulation of the tableau can take place.

Whenever play comes to a standstill thereafter, and provided all spaces are filled, a further ten cards are dealt face up to the foot of each column. After the initial tableau has been laid out, there will be five such further deals to the tableau (because there are initially 50 cards in the stock). If at the end of the final deal there is a card short or a card over, there has been a misdeal somewhere during the game.

Strategy This is a game which can move slowly at first, but if it gets into a rhythm, and spaces occur, can come with a run at the end. A priority is to try to create spaces by transferring elsewhere all the cards in a column. This gives the opportunity to move cards or suit sequences which might be blocking progress elsewhere to the spaces. When building from one column to another, try to build in suit sequences, since these can be moved wholesale. Sometimes spaces can be used to shuffle cards around into suit sequences.

Example game
The initial tableau is shown opposite. The ♥3 can be built on ♥4. The ♦9 can be built on ♦10, and ♦8 built on that. The ♠8 can be built on ♣9, and ♠5 on ♥6 with ♣4 on that. This leaves six cards at the foot of columns to be exposed and become available for play. Furthermore, when this is done the three right-hand columns will have only three face-down cards in each. When the cards exposed have been built and others exposed it may be that the extreme right-hand columns are on the way to being cleared. When no further moves can be made in the initial tableau, the stock is picked up and one face-up card is played to the foot of each of the ten columns, and the manipulation begins again. And so on…

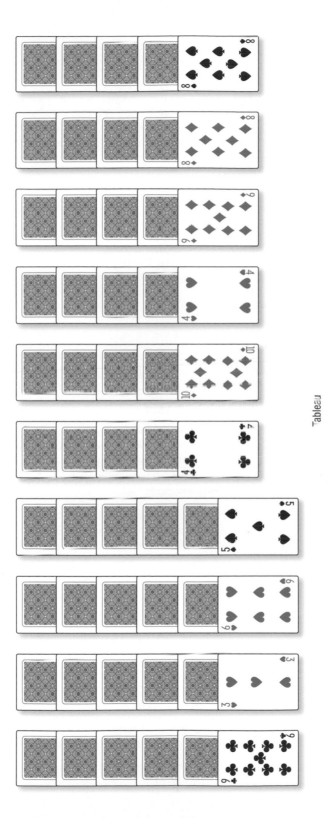

Tableau

137

Sultan

Sultan is a colourful patience game, the object of which is to reproduce a harem. A successful game ends with the ♥K (the Sultan) in masculine isolation surrounded by eight piles headed by Queens. The piles are built up from cards from the 'divan'. Excitable players are warned that the game is more often than not crowned with success.

Alternative names	(rarely) Emperor of Germany, Sultan of Turkey
Number of packs required	Two
Time needed to get it out	Twelve minutes
Prospects of success	About two in three

Aim
To end with the ♥K surrounded on all sides by eight piles of cards, all built in suit sequence up to Queens.

Preparation
The eight Kings and the ♥A are removed from the two packs and placed in three rows of three, with one ♥K in the centre, and the ♥A below it. It is convenient to place the other ♥K in the top centre, with the other three King suits in pairs down either side (see illustration). With the exception of the centre King, these cards are foundations, to be built up in ascending suit sequence to the Queens, with Aces following Kings and preceding 2s.

The combined pack is then shuffled, and the first eight cards are dealt in two columns of four, by tradition lengthwise to visually represent divans, one column each side of the foundations. The whole group, which in other games might be called the reserve, is called the divan.

Play
All cards of the divan are available to play to the foundations. When a card is played to a foundation from the divan, it is replaced by the top card of the waste heap, but not necessarily at once – if the player does not like the top card of the waste heap, he can await a more promising one.

When all possible moves have been made after the initial deal, the stock is turned one card at a time, and those cards that cannot be played to a foundation are played to a single waste heap, the top card of which is always available.

When the whole stock is dealt, two redeals of the waste heap are allowed. Unusually for patience games, a shuffle is allowed before each redeal.

Strategy The privilege of being able to reject a card to fill a space in the divan is valuable to a player who can remember what cards are buried in the waste heap. For example, if a foundation is built up to a 5, and both 6s are buried, it is pointless playing a 7 or higher to the divan. It is better to wait a card or two for a better prospect.

Example game

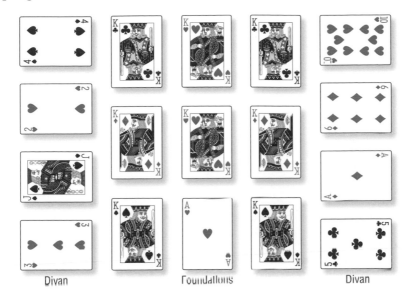

Divan   Foundations   Divan

The illustration shows an initial layout. Immediately, three cards from the divan can be played to the foundations: the ♦A to one of the ♦Ks, and the ♥2, 3 to ♥A. The player now begins to turn the cards from the stock one at a time to a waste heap, from where he can refill the three spaces in the divan either immediately or, if he prefers, later, provided he always uses the top card of the waste heap.

Variants

Some modern descriptions of this game comply with the usual rules of patience and insist that a space in the divan must be filled immediately by the top card of the waste heap, and that between deals the waste heap cannot be reshuffled but merely turned over and redealt. This book prefers to stick with tradition.

Tournament

Tournament is an improvement on an old patience game called La Nivernaise or Napoleon's Flank. It has its own vocabulary. There is room for skill.

Alternative names	None, but see above
Number of packs required	Two
Time needed to get it out	20 minutes
Prospects of success	About one in six

Aim

To end with eight piles, two for each suit, four built up in ascending sequence from Ace to King and four in descending sequence from King to Ace.

Preparation

The two packs are shuffled together, and two columns of four cards are dealt. These are the 'kibitzers', and act as a reserve (see illustration on p142). It is essential that at least one Ace or King is among the kibitzers (the game is practically impossible otherwise), so if none appears, the cards should be picked up, reshuffled and dealt again.

Space is left between the kibitzers for the 'dormitzers', the game's specific word for the tableau. The dormitzers are six columns of four cards, all dealt face up, with the cards in the columns overlapping each other.

Above the dormitzers is space for two rows of four foundation cards, one row for a King of each suit and one for the corresponding Aces. Kings and Aces are played to their position as they become available in play. It does not matter which row is which, but the Ace of a particular suit should be played above or below the King of its suit.

All kibitzers and all fully exposed dormitzers (ie those at the foot of the columns) are available for play. As they become available, Aces and Kings are played to the foundations and are built on in ascending and descending sequence respectively.

When a kibitzer is played its space is filled by any available dormitzer card, but not necessarily immediately. The space can be preserved for as long as the player wishes.

A space in the dormitzers caused by a whole column being played is filled by four new cards being dealt from stock (except after the final deal, when no further stock is left; the space then remains empty).

When all possible moves have been made, another four overlapping rows of six cards are dealt to the dormitzers, adding to the length of the columns. Play then proceeds as before, and when it comes to a standstill four more rows are added to the dormitzers. This continues until the stock is exhausted. It may be that on the last deal the stock contains fewer than the 24 cards required, in which case the cards are dealt in rows as far as they will go.

When the two foundations of a suit meet (eg if the Ace is built up to the 6, and the King down to the 7), a reversal rule applies. Any or all of the cards from one foundation may be reversed onto the other, including the Ace or King at the bottom of the pile.

When all the cards have been dealt and play is at a standstill, two redeals are allowed. The kibitzers remain in place, and the dormitzer piles are picked up, the first being placed face up on the second, the combined pile face up on the third, and so on to the end, so that when the combined stock is turned face down for redealing, the cards from the last column will be dealt first. No shuffling is allowed.

Strategy Spaces in the kibitzers are valuable, and ideally should not be filled until doing so will create a space elsewhere. Try not to fill a kibitzer space with a card that cannot be built to the foundations for a long time.

Use the reversal rule when it will help to release a vital card buried in the dormitzers. This may entail leaving the meeting foundations as they are for a while rather than disturbing the balance by playing an additional card to one or other foundation.

Try not to disturb meeting foundations just before the final redeal, when it is also advantageous to have as many spaces as possible among the kibitzers.

Example game
The cards are dealt as in the illustration overleaf.

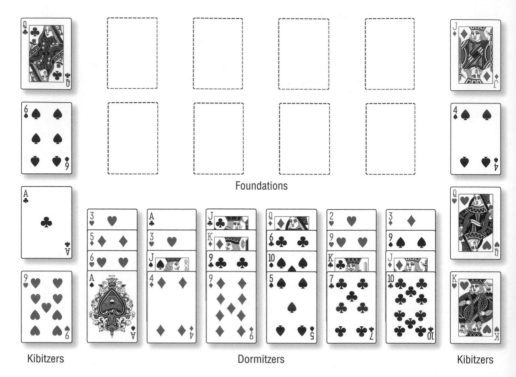

Foundations

Kibitzers   Dormitzers   Kibitzers

The ♣A and ♥K can be played immediately to foundation places from the kibitzers, as can ♠A from the first dormitzer column. The ♥Q can be played to the foundation on the ♥K, leaving three spaces in the kibitzers. The ♣7 can be played from the dormitzer column to a space in the kibitzers. This releases the ♣K to be played to the foundation, and the ♣Q to be built on it from the kibitzers, which restores the number of spaces in the kibitzers to three. It would now be useful to play the ♦9 and ♣9 from the dormitzers to the kibitzers, since this releases the ♦K to the foundations and the ♣J to be built on ♣Q. This empties a column of dormitzers, which is refilled with four new cards from the stock. This might allow other profitable moves to be made. Otherwise, four more rows are dealt from the stock to the existing dormitzer columns.

Vacancies

Vacancies is a rather mechanical patience game which requires a lot of space. However it is worth trying, and has the merit of rewarding care and concentration. It is difficult to get out, and not for the easily frustrated.

Alternative names	Gaps, Spaces
Number of packs required	One
Time needed to get it out	Ten minutes
Prospects of success	About 1 in 25

Aim

To arrange the pack so that each row is made up of cards of the same suit, ranging in sequence from 2 on the left to King on the right.

Preparation

The cards rank from 2 (low) to King (high). Aces play no significant part in the game.

The cards are shuffled and the whole pack is dealt face up in four rows, each of 13 cards, forming the tableau.

Play

From the tableau the four Aces are removed and set to one side. They play no part in the game.

Removing the Aces creates four spaces in the tableau. A space can be filled by one card only: the card of the same suit as that on the left of the space but of one rank higher. Thus, if ♦4 has a space to its right, the space can be filled only by ♦5.

The transfer of each card creates another space to be filled. By this means, cards are moved around the tableau one by one, and the object is to so manoeuvre the cards so that each row comprises 2 to King in a single suit sequence. It does not matter which suit fills which row, but once a row is started with 2 at the left it cannot be moved elsewhere.

However, there is a limit to what one can achieve, because if a space occurs to the right of a King, nothing can be moved there, there being no card one rank higher than a King. At the beginning, if none of the Aces to be removed is to the right of a King, there are four spaces to fill and four cards which might fill them. The skill lies in trying to avoid for as long as possible creating a space to the right of a King, which reduces the number of spaces operable to three.

Even the cleverest player will not be able to avoid this for long, and only with exceptional luck will it be possible to avoid eventually all four spaces being to the right of Kings, and thus useless.

However, the game does not end there. When this situation arises, all the cards which are not in their correct places are picked up, shuffled and redealt. The four spaces left on the redeal are the spaces in each row to the right of the cards which are in their proper places. If one or more of the rows does not yet have even the 2 in its final position (and this is not uncommon), then the space in that row is left at the end of the row, in the space reserved for the 2. This means that after the redeal there will be four spaces vacant and each is ready to accept the card which should be there if the game is to be got out. If at the time of the redeal one row has been completed from 2 to King, obviously no cards from that row are picked up and when the cards are redealt there will be only three spaces to leave (this is because in the completed row, the space is actually there, to the right of the King).

When the game is once more stopped by all the spaces being to the right of Kings, one more redeal is allowed, following the principles of the first. After that, if all the cards aren't in their correct places, defeat must be conceded.

Example game

In the tableau at the start of the game as illustrated opposite (which has two Kings together, which can be a help), ♣6 can be played to ♣5; then ♥5 to ♥4; ♠2 to the space left by moving the ♥5, followed by ♠3; ♦2 to the space at the left of the bottom row; ♥Q to ♥J; ♥6 to ♥5, allowing another 2 to be played to the space, and so on.

Tableau

Vanishing Cross

Vanishing Cross is probably the most popular name for this game, although it is one of the many patience games which carries the rank of a titled lady as an alternative name, in this case Czarina. It is not an easy game to get out.

Alternative names	Corner Card, Czarina, Four Seasons
Number of packs required	One
Time needed to get it out	Six minutes
Prospects of success	About one in twelve

Aim
To end with four piles of cards in ascending suit sequence upon their foundations.

Preparation
The cards are shuffled and five are dealt in the form of a cross to form a tableau. The next card is dealt to the top left corner of the cross. This card is the first foundation. The remaining cards are taken in hand, face down, as the stock.

Play
The rank of the foundation card determines the rank of the other three foundations. As they become available, they are played to the other corners of the tableau. They are built on in ascending suit sequence 'round-the-corner', meaning that when the King is the top card of the pile it will be followed by Ace.

Cards in the tableau (ie the cross) can be packed on in downward sequence irrespective of suit and colour. These sequences are also round-the-corner, so in this case King is packed on Ace. All the exposed cards in the tableau are available for play. They can be moved only one at a time; sequences cannot be transferred.

When all possible moves have been made in the initial tableau, cards are turned over one by one from the stock and played to a foundation or the tableau if possible. If not, they are played to a single waste heap. The card on top of the waste heap is always available for play. The stock is dealt only once. A space in the tableau can be filled by a card from the tableau, the waste heap or the stock.

Example game

In the illustration that follows, the tableau cross has been dealt and ♣9 is the first foundation.

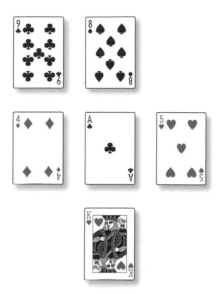

The ♦4 can be packed on the ♥5 and the ♥K on the ♣A. The first card is then turned from the stock and played to a foundation, a card in the tableau or to one of the spaces, then the next and so on.

The main thing to remember is that foundations are built up and tableau cards are packed down.

Weavers

Weavers is an unusual and frequently infuriating game because although it occupies the player for a pleasant 20 minutes or so, it has a habit of getting blocked close to the end. It is a game of luck.

Alternative names	Leoni's Own
Number of packs required	Two
Time needed to get it out	20 minutes
Prospects of success	About one in eight

Aim

To finish with four piles of cards built in ascending suit sequence from Ace up to King, and four piles in descending suit sequence from King to Ace.

Preparation

Four Aces and four Kings, one from each suit, are arranged in a line at the top of table as foundation cards.

The two packs are shuffled thoroughly together and a row of 13 face-up cards is dealt from left to right. In practice, it is convenient to have two rows, one of six and one of seven cards, imagining them as continuous. The whole pack is then dealt, face up, one at a time upon these rows until it is exhausted. The 13 piles form the tableau.

While dealing, the player has to imagine that each pile represents a rank, from Ace at the left to King at the right, and while dealing should recite (out loud if so inclined) the rank of the pile to which he is dealing a card. If the card about to be dealt is of the rank of the pile it is destined for, it is put aside face down. It is an 'exile'. The deal continues with the next card being dealt to the same pile from which the previous card was exiled; no pile is missed. At the end of the deal there is usually a pile of half-a-dozen or so exiles.

Play

After the deal, the cards of the 13th, or King pile, are spread out. These form a reserve, and all these cards are available for play, as are any cards added to the reserve during play. The other cards available are the top cards of the remaining twelve piles.

Available cards are played to the foundations, in ascending suit sequence on the Aces, and descending on the Kings, and a card played from a tableau pile exposes the card beneath it, which becomes available.

When play is blocked, the top card of the exile pile is turned over. If it can be played to a foundation, then it must be (the player has no option). If it cannot, it is placed on the bottom of the tableau representing its rank, and the top card of the tableau pile removed. It too is played to the bottom of the pile representing its rank, and the top card removed, and so on. This process is called 'shifting'.

As soon as a card removed from a pile exposes a card that can be played to a foundation, another spell of building begins. The card lifted from the pile is placed beneath its own pile, and the card exposed is played to its foundation. The shifting around of the cards might now allow other cards to be played to the foundations. When all such moves have been made, and the game is again at a standstill, the next card in the exile pile is turned over and play begins again.

When a card taken from the exile pile, or taken from the top of a tableau pile in the course of shifting, is a King, it is played to the King pile, or reserve, and that spell of shifting comes to an end, even if the card exposed by the King is playable to a foundation. Play must restart with the next card from the exile pile being turned.

One further tactic allowed occurs when the two foundation piles of a suit meet, eg when the Ace foundation is built up to 6 and the King foundation is built down to 7. In this case any number of cards (except the foundation Aces and Kings) may be played from one pile to the other. This can sometimes enable a run of cards to be played from the tableau. When the two piles meet, the rule whereby an exile card must be played directly to the foundation if possible is waived. If the exile card would upset the 'match' of the two foundation piles, the player is allowed to play it to the foot of the pile representing its rank to begin a further shifting.

When play is blocked for any reason, the deal comes to an end. Two redeals are allowed. The new stock is made by picking up the King pile face up, placing the Queen pile face up upon it, and so on down to the Ace pile. Unused exile cards, if any remain, are placed face up on the Ace pile. When the pile is turned over for redealing, the first cards dealt will therefore be the cards previously in the King pile.

Example game
The illustration overleaf shows the layout when the cards are first dealt.

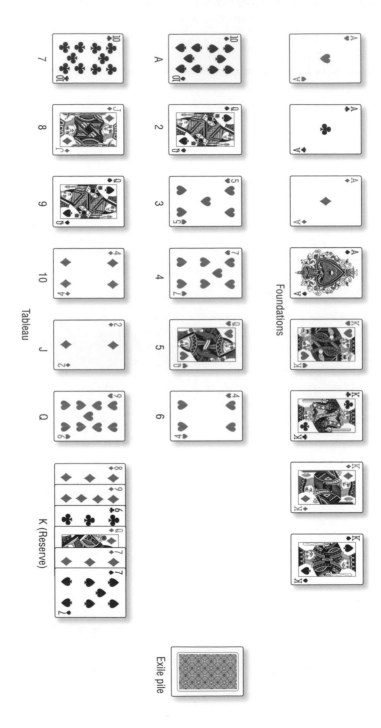

Foundations

Tableau

K (Reserve)

Exile pile

The foundations, tableau and exile pile are in place. The tableau piles have been numbered for explanation to show the rank of card they represent. In normal play the player must keep these in mind. The King pile has been spread, and is the reserve.

One of the ♠Qs is played to the foundation, as is the ♥Q, the ♦2, and the ♦Q from the reserve. This last allows the ♦J to be played to the foundation. When any other plays made possible by new cards being exposed have been made, the top card is turned over from the exile pile, and the first shifting operation begins.

Wheel of Fortune

Wheel of Fortune is a game that requires some skill and concentration. It features two vital concessions at the end that give the player extra chances to succeed in a patience which does not come out very often.

Alternative names	None
Number of packs required	Two
Time needed to get it out	25 minutes
Prospects of success	About one in eight

Aim
To build each suit in two piles, one on Ace foundations up to Kings, and the other on King foundations down to Aces.

Preparation
Each pack should be thoroughly shuffled separately. They should not be amalgamated as one pack is used before the other.

Play
One pack is put aside and the other taken in hand. Sixteen cards are dealt clockwise in a large circle or wheel, beginning at top centre (ie '12 o'clock'), leaving enough space in the middle for four Aces and four Kings to be arranged in two columns as foundation cards, as in the illustration. The wheel is the tableau.

All 16 cards in the wheel are available for play. Any Aces and Kings dealt among them are played to the centre as foundations; Aces are placed in the left-hand column and their matching Kings in the right-hand column.

As each card is played to the foundation, the space in the tableau is filled from the hand by dealing the top card from the stock. Once a foundation card is played to the centre, available cards can be built upon it in suit sequence, upwards on the Aces and downwards on the Kings, with each space being refilled immediately from the stock.

When play comes to a standstill and no more moves can be made, 16 more cards are added to the 16 in the tableau, beginning at the top centre of the wheel as before. Cards cannot be played to the foundations during the deal, but when it is complete, available cards are again built on foundations, the playing of a card making the one below it available. If a space occurs through all the cards in the pile being played to foundations, it is filled immediately by a single card from the stock, as before.

When play again comes to a standstill, the dealing of 16 more cards is repeated. When the first pack of cards is exhausted, the second is taken in hand to replace it and play continues without a break. Obviously, by now, all the foundation cards will be in place, so Aces and Kings in the second pack are not used as foundations, but will, if the game is successful, eventually top all the foundation piles.

Play continues in this manner, except that the final deal of cards is likely to be fewer than 16 and therefore may not complete the circle.

If play comes to a standstill after the final deal, and there are no further cards in hand, there are two more aids to getting the patience out. Firstly, if the two foundation piles of the same suit meet in sequence (eg the Ace is built up to 7 and the King down to 8) any number of cards including, if desired, the foundation cards themselves, can be transferred from one pile to the other, providing the correct sequence is maintained. By this means, an available card or cards might become playable from the wheel to the foundation, thus allowing further moves.

As a last resort, if a space occurs in the wheel after the stock is exhausted it can be filled by any available card from elsewhere in the wheel. At this stage it is legitimate to spread the piles slightly so that the player can see which cards are below the top card. He can then play a card to the space that will expose a card which can be played to a foundation and get the game moving again.

Example game
The illustration overleaf shows the layout when the cards are first dealt.

Foundations

Aces   Kings

Tableau

One shuffled pack is taken in hand face down as the stock and 16 cards are dealt from it. The ♦K is played to its foundation and replaced by the top card of the stock. The ♣K follows similarly as does the ♦A.

The ♣Q and ♦2, 3, 4 can be built to their foundations, each one being replaced by the top card of the stock as it is played. It may be that some of the replacement cards can be played to their foundations, in which case they in turn will be replaced from the stock.

When no further building can be made, no matter how many cards have been built to the foundations, there will remain a wheel of 16 cards around them. Sixteen more cards are now added to the wheel and the process repeated. The game proceeds as described above.

Windmill

Windmill is so-called because its tableau resembles the four sails of a windmill; it is also known as Propeller, as its four arms are reminiscent of the blades of a propeller. Windmill is a simple game in which luck plays the biggest part.

Alternative names	Propeller
Number of packs required	Two
Time needed to get it out	Six minutes
Prospects of success	One in twelve

Aim

To finish with a central pile of 52 cards, built up in four successive descending King to Ace sequences, surrounded by four piles of 13 cards built up in ascending Ace to King sequences.

Preparation

Any King is selected from the two packs and placed in the centre of the table. The two packs are shuffled together and taken in hand face down.

Play

Two cards are dealt face up in a column above the King, two are dealt below it, and two are dealt in a row to the right and two to the left of it.

The central King is the main foundation, and the eight cards forming the 'sails' of the windmill form the tableau. All cards in the tableau are available for play. The object is to build on the King a descending round-the-corner sequence of 52 cards, regardless of suit or colour, with King following Ace. The completed pile will be topped by the fourth Ace.

Meanwhile, as Aces become available, they are played to positions at the angles of the sails to become foundations themselves, which are built up in four ascending sequences, again regardless of suit or colour, to Kings. A card taken from the tableau to be built on a foundation is replaced immediately by the top card of a waste heap, or if none exists, the top card from the hand.

When all possible moves have been made after the initial deal, the cards in hand (the stock) are turned one at a time and played to a foundation, if possible, or if not to a single waste heap. The top card of the waste heap is always available for play. At any time, the top card from an Ace foundation may be transferred to the central King foundation if it continues the sequence, but only one card at a time can be transferred; it is necessary for the next card played to the King foundation to come from elsewhere before another card from the same Ace foundation can be used.

If the stock becomes exhausted, while cards remain in the waste heap, the game is not immediately lost. There is no complete redeal of the waste heap, but it can be turned over and redealt for as long as the cards dealt can be played to the foundations or are needed to fill the tableau. Otherwise the game is lost.

Strategy Advantage should be taken of the rule which allows a card from an Ace foundation to be transferred to the King foundation, as this will sometimes allow the top card of the waste heap also to be played to the King foundation, when otherwise it would not be available. Always build cards to the King foundation, although it is often better not to play a card from the tableau to an Ace foundation if the card from the waste heap which would replace it will duplicate a rank already in the tableau. It is best to keep as many ranks as possible in the tableau, or topping the Ace foundations, in order to supply the King foundation, and sometimes it is worth delaying the moving of a card from the tableau to an Ace foundation in the hope that the next card turned from the stock to the waste heap would be a better replacement for it.

Example game

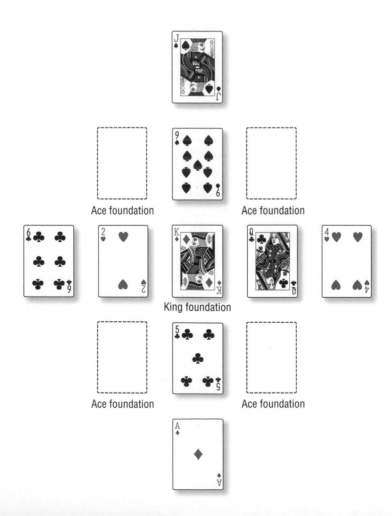

The illustration shows the tableau after the initial deal. The ♣Q can be built on to the central ♦K foundation, followed by the ♠J. The ♦A can be played to one of the four foundation places within the sails of the windmill, and the ♥2 built on it. The four spaces thus created in the sails may be filled from the stock, there being no waste heap as yet, and this might enable further building. When nothing more can be done, the first card is turned from the stock, and play proceeds as described.

Card Games Glossary

The glossary does not include game names or variants, for which the index can be consulted.

available card a card in a tableau which is in a position from where it can legally be played to a foundation or elsewhere, or where another card can be packed on it

bed in Flower Garden, one of the six rows of six cards that form part of the tableau

blocked card a card in the tableau situated so that it cannot be moved to a foundation until another card blocking it is moved first, while at the same time the card blocking it cannot itself be moved to a foundation until the original blocked card is moved; the situation must be resolved by play within the tableau

blocked column or **row** a column or row containing a blocked card

bouquet in Flower Garden, a crescent of 16 cards that forms part of the tableau

build to transfer cards to foundations

card one of a pack, usually of 52 cards, divided into four suits used in playing games

court card the King, Queen or Jack of each suit

face card same as court card

grace card in Limited, one of the four cards from the waste pile that become available for play when all other options have been exhausted

picture card same as court card

plain card a card other than a court card

upcard the top card of a pile, turned face up

clubs (♣) one of the four customary suits of playing cards, comprising 13 cards with black trefoil pips

colour the colour of the pips and characters on a card: red for diamonds and hearts, black for spades and clubs

column a number of cards in the tableau arranged one above the other, either separated from each other or overlapping (*see also* row)

deal the act of distributing or laying out cards

deck *same as* pack

diamonds (♦) one of the four customary suits of playing cards, comprising 13 cards with red diamond-shaped pips

discard to throw away a card or cards, as not needed or not allowed by the game; the act of discarding

divan in Sultan, the name for the reserve (*see* reserve)

dormitzers in Tournament, the name for the cards in the tableau

exile pile in Weavers, cards temporarily put aside, face down, during the deal, to be used at a later stage of play

exposed card (*a*) a card which is dealt at the bottom of a column or right of a fan, or which otherwise may be played on or moved subject to the rules of the game (*b*) a card in the tableau which is revealed when a card covering it is played, and which therefore becomes available for play itself (*c*) a face-down card is said to be exposed when it is turned face up

face the printed side of a playing card that shows its pip value, as opposed to the back

face down with the side of the card that displays the pip value hidden

face up with the side of the card that displays the pip value visible

fan cards arranged in a crescent shape, with each card overlapping another, so that the rank and suit of each is visible; in games using three-card fans in the tableau, the crescent shape is often ignored, and the cards overlap in a row

foundation a card which is separated from the pack or tableau and upon which a whole suit or sequence must be built

foundation pile the pile of cards which have been played to a foundation

get out to win a patience game by achieving the aim of the game

grace card *see under* card

hearts (♥) one of the four customary suits of playing cards, comprising 13 cards with red heart-shaped pips

heel in Demon, the name for the cards in the reserve

index cards in As You Like It, the row of cards which remind the player of the ranks of the corresponding foundation cards, and thus indicate when a foundation pile is complete

kibitzers in Tournament, the name for the cards in the reserve

layout the arrangement of cards upon the table

pack a complete set of playing cards, usually comprising 52 cards

packing the placing of one tableau card onto another, usually in sequence according to the rules, and usually overlapping, so that the player can see the whole sequence

pair two cards of the same rank

patience a card game for one (called 'solitaire' in North America)

pip a suit symbol spot on a card

pip value the total of the pips on a playing card, for example a 3 card has a pip value of 3

post in Gate, one of the two upright columns of cards in the tableau, the bottom one of which is available

rails in Gate, the two rows of available cards in the tableau

rank the grade or position of a particular card in its suit, for example 3, 10 and Jack are ranks

release to make a card available for play (usually by playing the cards blocking it)

reserve cards that are available for play which are not part of the foundations, stock, tableau or discard piles

reversing the practice sometimes allowed in two-pack patiences where sequences are built simultaneously, ascending on Ace foundations and descending on King foundations, whereby when the top cards of two foundations are in sequence (eg the Ace foundation is built up to 6 and the King foundation down to 7) cards may be transferred from one foundation to the other

round-the-corner *see* round-the-corner sequence *under* sequence

row a horizontal line of cards running from left to right, either separated or overlapping (*see also* column)

sequence a set of two or more cards consecutive in value

ascending sequence a sequence in which cards run up, for example from 2 to King

descending sequence a sequence in which cards run down, for example from King to 2

round-the-corner sequence the continuous sequence of cards in which Ace ranks between King and 2, as in the ascending sequence Queen, King, Ace, 2, 3 and the descending sequence 3, 2, Ace, King, Queen

suit sequence a sequence in which the cards are all of the same suit

shuffle to mix cards at random

solitaire the North American term for games of patience

spades (♠) one of the four customary suits of playing cards, comprising 13 cards with black shovel-like pips

stock the undealt part of a pack of cards, which may be used later in the deal

suit one of the sets of cards of the same denomination: clubs, diamonds, hearts or spades

tableau the main part of the layout of cards on the table

talon *same as* waste heap

terrace in Queen of Italy, the name for the cards in the reserve

waiving in Miss Milligan, the option, after all cards in the stock have run out, to take into the hand temporarily an exposed card which is blocking play

waste heap or **waste pile** the pile of cards that could not be played either to a foundation or to an exposed card in the tableau

worrying-back the privilege, rare but allowed in some games, of playing a card from a foundation back into the tableau

Index

Games by Alternative Names

Aces Up *see* Easthaven **45**
Alexander the Great *see* La Belle
   Lucie **73**
Alliance *see* Betsy Ross **16**

Big Forty *see* Le Cadran **82**
Bouquet *see* Flower Garden **49**
Broken Intervals *see* Calculation **26**

Canfield *see* Demon **38**; Klondike **71**
Clover Leaf *see* La Belle Lucie **73**
Corner Card *see* Vanishing Cross **146**
Czarina *see* Vanishing Cross **146**

Double and Quits *see* Monte
   Carlo **101**
Double Klondike *see* Gargantua **57**

Eight Away *see* Eight Off **47**
Emperor of Germany *see* Sultan **138**

Fan *see* La Belle Lucie **73**
Fascination *see* Klondike **71**
Firing Squad *see* Aces Up **5**
Five Piles *see* Baroness **13**
Forty Thieves *see* Le Cadran **82**
Four Kings *see* Betsy Ross **16**
Four Seasons *see* Vanishing
   Cross **146**
Fourteens *see* Fourteen Out **52**

Gaps *see* Vacancies **143**
Glenwood *see* Duchess **41**
Good Measure *see* Baker's Dozen
   (variant) **10**
Grand Duchess *see* Duchess de
   Luynes **43**

Harp *see* Gargantua **57**

Idiot's Delight *see* King Albert **68**

Idle Year *see* Accordion **3**

King's Audience *see* Queen's
   Audience (variant) **120**

La Nivernaise *see* Tournament **140**
Laying Siege *see* Beleaguered
   Castle **14**
Leoni's Own *see* Weavers **148**

Methuselah *see* Accordion **3**
Midnight Oil *see* La Belle Lucie **73**
Musical Patience *see* Betsy Ross **16**

Napoleon at St Helena *see* Le
   Cadran **82**
Napoleon's Favourite *see* St
   Helena **129**
Napoleon's Flank *see*
   Tournament **140**
Narcotic *see* Perpetual Motion **113**

Old Patience *see* Sir Tommy **133**

Parallels *see* British Blockade **21**
Parisian *see* Duchess de Luynes
   (variant) **43**
Parisienne *see* Duchess de Luynes
   (variant) **43**
Pile of Twenty-eight *see*
   Pyramid **115**
Propeller *see* Windmill **155**

Quadruple *see* Betsy Ross **16**

Rouge et Noir *see* Red and Black **122**

Sham Battle *see* Beleaguered
   Castle **14**
Signora *see* Queen of Italy **117**
Spaces *see* Vacancies **143**

Sultan of Turkey *see* Sultan **138**
Sundial *see* Clock **33**

Take Fourteen *see* Fourteen Out **52**
Terrace *see* Queen of Italy **117**
The Garden *see* Flower Garden **49**
Thirteen *see* Demon **38**
Thirteens *see* Baroness **13**
Toad *see* Frog **55**

Toad-in-the-Hole *see* Frog **55**
Travellers *see* Clock **33**
Treasure Trove *see* Osmosis **110**
Triangle *see* Klondike **71**
Try Again *see* Sir Tommy **133**

Washington's Favourite *see* St
 Helena **129**
Wedding *see* Monte Carlo **101**

Games by Number of Packs

One Pack

Accordion 3
Aces Up 5
Baker's Dozen 10
Baroness 13
Beleaguered Castle 14
Betsy Ross 16
Bisley 17
Bristol 19
Calculation 26
Captive Queens 29
Castles in Spain 31
Clock 33
Crossword 35
Demon 38
Duchess 41
Easthaven 45
Eight Off 47
Flower Garden 49
Fourteen Out 52

Friday the Thirteenth 53
Gate 60
Grandfather's Clock 63
King Albert 68
Klondike 71
La Belle Lucie 73
Little Spider 90
Martha 93
Monte Carlo 101
One Foundation 108
Osmosis 110
Pas Seul 112
Perpetual Motion 113
Pyramid 115
Queen's Audience 120
Rosamund's Bower 124
Sir Tommy 133
Vacancies 143
Vanishing Cross 146

Two Packs

As You Like It 7
British Blockade 21
British Square 24
Duchess de Luynes 43
Frog 55
Gargantua 57
Herringbone 65
Lady of the Manor 76
Lady Palk 79
Le Cadran 82
Legitimist 85
Limited 87
Matrimony 96
Miss Milligan 98

Mount Olympus 103
Odd and Even 106
Queen of Italy 117
Red and Black 122
Royal Rendezvous 127
St Helena 129
Salic Law 131
Spider 135
Sultan 138
Tournament 140
Weavers 148
Wheel of Fortune 152
Windmill 155

Chambers & Card Games

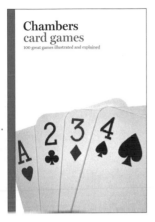

Chambers Card Games

Chambers Card Games is a comprehensive and fun guide to 100 varied card games, suitable for players of all ages and for any occasion. As well as providing detailed instructions, strategies and tips, this fully-illustrated book also features a history of card games and the stories behind the court cards.

Whether you're playing cards alone or with friends and family, for profit or just for pleasure, this book contains everything you need to know for hours of entertainment.

Price: £9.99   *ISBN: 978 0550 10336 9*
Paperback   *420 pages*

Chambers Pocket Card Games

This compact new collection features dozens of great card games, with clear instructions backed up by illustrations, strategies and handy hints, as well as practical information to help novice players get started. From bezique on the beach to patience on the plane, *Chambers Pocket Card Games* is an ideal travel companion as well as a useful home reference.

Price: £5.99   *ISBN: 978 0550 10408 3*
Paperback   *288 pages*

Chambers Card Games for Gambling

Whether you're playing for big bucks or just for pennies, *Chambers Card Games for Gambling* teaches you everything you need to know to play and win at cards. From high-stakes Baccarat to family-friendly Red Dog, this new collection includes fun games you can play at home as well as casino games requiring serious skill and a poker face. Detailed instructions for each game are complemented by illustrated examples and strategies for success.

Price: £5.99   *ISBN: 978 0550 10408 3*
Paperback   *176 pages*

Visit www.chambers.co.uk for further details, or call
0131 556 5929 for a Chambers catalogue.

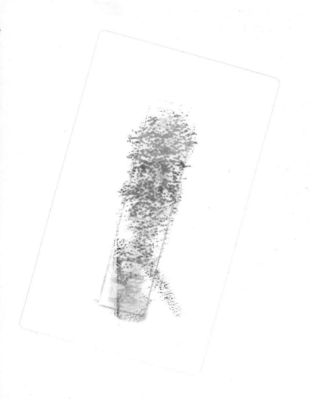